BRAIN-BASED TEACHING FOR ALL SUBJECTS

Patterns to Promote Learning

Madlon T. Laster

Rowman & Littlefield Education
Lanham, Maryland • Toronto • Plymouth, UK
2008

Published in the United States of America
by Rowman & Littlefield Education
A Division of Rowman & Littlefield Publishers, Inc.
A wholly owned subsidary of The Rowman & Littlefield Publishing Group, Inc.
4501 Forbes Boulevard, Suite 200, Lanham, Maryland 20706
www.rowmaneducation.com

Estover Road
Plymouth PL6 7PY
United Kingdom

British Library Cataloguing in Publication Information Available

Library of Congress Cataloging-in-Publication Data
Laster, Madlon T., 1935–
   Brain-based teaching for all subjects : patterns to promote learning / Madlon
T. Laster.
      p. cm.
   Includes bibliographical references.
   ISBN-13: 978-1-57886-721-9 (alk. paper)
   ISBN-10: 1-57886-721-5 (alk. paper)
   ISBN-13: 978-1-57886-722-6 (pbk. : alk. paper)
   ISBN-10: 1-57886-722-3 (pbk. : alk. paper)
   1. Learning, Psychology of. 2. Cognitive learning. 3. Teaching–Psychological
aspects. 4. Brain. I. Title.
   LB1060.L37 2008
   370.15–dc22   2007033502

∞™ The paper used in this publication meets the minimum requirements of
American National Standard for Information Sciences—Permanence of Paper
for Printed Library Materials, ANSI/NISO Z39.48-1992.
Manufactured in the United States of America.

This effort is dedicated to Dr. Joan Fulton,
who inspired my last seventeen years of teaching with her
instructional approach based on brain research.

Special thanks go to my husband,
Dr. James H. Laster, who made me think this book could be
accomplished and helped smooth the hurdles along the way.
It would not have happened without him.

CONTENTS

LIST OF ILLUSTRATIONS

FOREWORD

From the beginning of time, humans have been curious and fascinated about how their brains work. Many of their assumptions were incorrect, and we've been saddled with misconceptions of this three-pound universe within our skull. A new day has dawned with the advent of brain-imaging technologies. Neuroscience research over the past two decades has resulted in an explosion of information about brain structure and function, greatly increasing our understanding not only of diseases of the brain, but also of how the brain takes in and encodes information: how we learn.

For educators this new information has great import. The human brain is what we teach, and we've had little information about how it works. Past practice has been based on the behaviorist tradition, but the positive reinforcement this theory espouses doesn't always work. Teachers have had to rely on their own best sense of what worked—their intuition. This doesn't mean that teachers haven't done a good job. Many have been very effective; but in many cases, the teachers weren't certain why their methods worked and, therefore, strategies were seldom shared with others in the profession. In other words, we have not been a profession that has had the background, training, or an accepted theory of learning to be articulate about our craft.

The research coming out of the neurosciences and cognitive science has the potential to move the profession from folklore to science. While scientists seldom conduct research on teaching strategies, general findings are emerging that are helping us to understand why certain methodologies and strategies are effective. The classroom has become a laboratory where teachers can begin to look at the research and to either understand why what they've been using worked or design methodologies that best match how the brain processes information effectively.

This book is an excellent example of both these options. Written by an experienced, effective teacher, it demonstrates in clear language how the strategies that she has used have produced excellent results and explains why they work based on her understanding of the research. She explains how these methodologies have increased both student understanding and retention of the information.

Whether teachers are helping kindergarten children understand the water cycle or assisting high school students to comprehend economic principles through a study of Shakespeare's *Merchant of Venice*, the author provides a variety of visual frameworks for organizing the information. Readers will be introduced to event-frames, the six dimensions of a complete description, culture boxes, and a host of other brain-compatible strategies.

Too often, when teachers retire, they take their secrets with them. They leave a mark on their students, but not on the profession. This author is an exception. The very valuable "secrets" designed and tested by her are here for the profession to employ. Both students and the profession will be the lucky recipients.

—Pat Wolfe, Ed.D.
—May 15, 2007

"Pat Wolfe is a former teacher of kindergarten through 12th grade, county office administrator, and adjunct university professor. Over the past twenty years, as an educational consultant, she has conducted workshops for thousands of administrators, teachers, boards of education, and parents in schools and districts throughout the United States and in over fifty countries internationally. Her major area of expertise is the application of brain research to educational practice. Her entertaining and interactive presentation style makes learning about the brain enjoyable, as well as practical. She is an award-winning author and has appeared on numerous videotape series, satellite broadcasts, radio shows, and television programs. Dr. Wolfe is a native of Missouri. She completed her undergraduate work in Oklahoma and her postgraduate studies in California. She presently resides in Napa, California."

—From Dr. Wolfe's web site: www.patwolfe.com

PREFACE: HOW THIS
ALL HAPPENED TO ME

It does not seem that long ago, but it was exactly fifty years ago, in September 1956, that I stepped into a classroom on the teacher's side of the desk. After forty-two years in the classroom, I am finding time to describe a visual approach to presenting new ideas to students, because no matter how much time goes by, babies, toddlers, children, and teens still must learn basic information and skills they will need throughout their lives. Technology, frequently, has changed the way we deliver that information, but evolution has not changed the manner in which the neurons of the brain connect with each other.

A national organization to help African-American students fund their college or university education has the familiar slogan: "A mind is a terrible thing to waste." I would put another twist on that: "A mind is a terrible thing to lose." But to read a lot of the humorous e-mail messaging that circulates through cyberspace these days, one might think that a lot of minds are being lost—not all at once, but gradually.

We all experience what we heard our parents say, "I better do it now before I forget," or "I came upstairs for something; what was it?" and we think, "Oh, no! I'm becoming my mother (or father)!" And then there are the conversational slips when the brain feeds the speaker a word the person did not intend to say. It is enough to make one wonder if the speed of losing brain cells hasn't increased, or perhaps the whole mind is going at once.

When it happened to me, I had been in the classroom for twenty-five years, and it wasn't comforting to begin to worry about my own brain instead of my students'. But the timing was curiously right. The research on learning and memory from a relatively new field called Cognitive Science was finding its way into ordinary periodicals, not just professional journals. I kept reading these articles to understand my own mind's changes, but was amazed at what research had discovered. I kept thinking that, if the brain works this way to take in and store information, then shouldn't someone be telling classroom teachers how to teach in a parallel way that would enhance learning and retention?

There it was—an article in the *Virginia Journal of Education,* back in the spring of 1983 or 1984, talking about Dr. Joan Fulton, a Piaget scholar, who had taken brain research and translated it into teaching strategies for the classroom. A workshop was scheduled at a Virginia lakeside conference center that fall, and I made sure I was there. Reading those emerging articles describing brain research for my own curiosity provided a background for the presentations at the conference. I understood quickly terms like *concept models* and *concept construction,* and the gist of what I began to call brain-based instruction. Today, I meet that phrase in many places.

By the summer of 1985, I was in a classroom at Radford University as a registered student listening to Dr. Fulton. What I learned there changed the way I taught for the remainder of my forty-two-year career.

I hope that the useful knowledge and techniques will help readers in their classrooms or parents with students at home. Some of the ideas are very simple; but, indeed, why be complicated when simple works? Other ideas may take some preparation and practice. Use the ones that suit your personal style. All involve basic discussions to involve students in thinking about the concepts. Once students have an understanding of those concepts, what you do in helping the students apply them will be your own creative approach to teaching.

One of the aspects of a career in teaching is that we sometimes do not know if we have had the positive influence on students for which we strive. Years can go by before we hear from a student who remembers the part we played in his or her life, and most of the others do not keep in touch with us, nor act on a memory they have of being in our classes. I have been very fortunate in having students and parents return to my school, or see me out in the community and share the successful results they have had in their further schooling, results which they attribute to these methods. May you find them valuable as well.

ACKNOWLEDGMENTS

It is a daunting prospect to acknowledge those to whom I owe such a great deal for the experienced successes in a long career, but family, professors, colleagues, and students all deserve recognition for making me the teacher that I became. To all those standing in the background of my past and present, I send my eternal gratitude.

Dr. Joan Fulton encouraged me in my intent to write the book, and gave her permission to reprint *Harold, Six Parts of a Description,* and her samples of four basic paragraphs. I could dedicate this book to none other.

A special word of thanks belongs to my husband, Dr. James H. Laster, for keeping me calm, encouraging me, and sharing his experiences with the publishing world. He also notated my mother's version of *Around the Corner,* the verb song, and preposition chant.

It was a treat to renew a connection with Dr. Pat Wolfe, who wrote the foreword for this book. She had come to Winchester, Virginia, some twenty years ago to share Dr. Madeline Hunter's *Elements of Effective Teaching,* and included brain research findings in her workshop. I am grateful for her approval of this effort of mine.

Two colleagues were like cheerleaders and consultants, both while I taught and while I was working on this project: N. Hartley Schearer and

Glenne White. Glenne read my third draft and made invaluable suggestions, as did Liza Bush, a former middle school student now teaching
seventh grade, and Dr. Kate Simpson of Lord Fairfax Community College.

For a book about using visual images to teach curriculum concepts, illustrations were vital, and they would not have been possible in this digital age without the consummate skill and innate understanding of my
graphics designer, Angela Lee, of Leeway Graphic Design, LLC.

I am also indebted to the Australian Embassy in Washington, D.C.,
for forwarding to the proper authorities my request to reprint the illustration for *G is for goanna* from the coloring book, originally published
by the Australian News and Information Bureau. The Australian Department of Foreign Affairs and Trade is the current holder of the copyright and generously granted their permission to reprint.

Finding the copyright holder for Watson and Nolte's *A Living Grammar* was daunting; all the various attempts led to a dead end. On the Internet, however, the original review of the book, as published by Webb
Publishing, was found as printed in an issue of *Time* magazine for September 26, 1938, including a few couplets from the "Parts of Speech
Poem."

I must also thank Rowman & Littlefield for offering me the chance to
take on this adventure, and to thank Sherry Glenn for her careful and
annotated editing.

INTRODUCTION

HOW DID BRAIN RESEARCH GET US HERE?

The art of teaching is the art of assisting discovery.

—Pablo Casals

To look back on the effects of latter day twentieth-century brain research, with its findings in cognitive science about learning and memory, storage, retention, and retrieval, is to see how the information attracted the interest of educators. Some people became names in the new field, and it was also interesting to see what twists they put on those discoveries.

One early title everyone discussed was *Left Brain, Right Brain* by Sally P. Springer and Georg Deutsch (1981). They reported on results of split-brain surgeries to help epileptics, operations that shed more light on how the brain worked, and how differently the two hemispheres responded to stimuli. Soon, workshop presenters at teachers' conferences were talking about being right- or left-brained and about hemispheric dominance. Often, they shared a checklist to help conferees determine their preferred hemisphere when faced with a problem or a choice in a course of action. In my lighter moods, I thought it sounded as though we all had only half a brain. Subsequent research shows whole-brain activity at all times.

Psychologists and theorists took this further to identify personality types, going beyond the familiar Myers-Briggs profiling tests of the 1950s, which had been based on the work of Carl G. Jung. You heard teachers saying, "I'm abstract-random," or "concrete-sequential," for example. They had gone through a set of questions about preferences in the way they worked, and determined where they landed on two intersecting continua between temperament opposites.

Educational ideas, like fashion styles, circulate in various translations, but as communication technology speeds up information sharing, we might observe that since 1960, each decade has seemed to have its popular theme: new math, creativity, problem-solving, thinking skills, and cooperative learning. Around 1980, educational concerns resulted in a "minimum competency" testing thrust, which—alas!—simply focused on the minimum a student needed to know to function successfully in the world of work. At the most recent turn-of-a-century, we picked up a testing focus with the well intentioned slogan of, "Leave no child behind." It was difficult to tell if any of these circling themes made good use of the way students' brains actually learned what they needed to know.

Lawrence Lowery, writing in the November 1998 issue of *Educational Leadership*, stated, "The only way the brain takes in data is through the sensory perceptions that enter through the windows of the body's five senses" (p. 26).

Jane Healy, Ph.D., (1987, 1990), educational psychologist, wrote two books: *Your Child's Growing Brain* and *Endangered Minds*. The latter particularly helped parents and teachers see how changes in the way society received information affected not only the way we learn, but the way the brain develops. Healy further explained that how we learn actually dictates how the brain wires itself. Each experience causes the neurons to connect with others, forming a neuron pathway of memory. Pathways that are used often become stronger and stronger, which creates more and more connections to other neurons.

The brain responds to specific incoming stimuli, and if the majority of it comes into the brain as visual information, the visual storage centers grow more, occupying more brain-space. Healy interviewed teachers, psychologists, and neurosurgeons in the United States and Europe, and felt secure in hypothesizing that the brains of students in the 1990s were literally different in structure than the brains of children in 1970 because of all the visual stimuli via video games, movies, and television—and also today, through their cell phones and more. (See note 1.)

A series of television programs called *Reading Rockets* has shared the ways children who are finding it difficult to learn to read can be tested and diagnosed, and then receive early intervention in cases of dyslexia, language delay, hearing problems, and autism. One program, aired on Washington, D.C.'s PBS channel 26, WETA, on September 3, 2006, showed a device (a net cap with electrical connections) that could be put on the head of a one-day-old infant to check whether the baby would have reading problems (www.readrockets.org/shows/brain). The electrical responses of the baby's brain to the sounds of b and p showed that the infant, less than twenty-four-hours-old, did hear the difference. Problems of phoneme-awareness and slow audio-processing have more chance of being corrected than ever.

With all of this research on learning and memory, brain function, and the warnings about the amount of visual bombardment that we receive these days (not to take up the topics of pollution, poor nutrition, and other variables), why haven't we made more of an effort to teach the way the brain learns? I did not have to wait long; professional journals addressed the subject. In 1984, the Corporation for Public Broadcasting received a grant from the Annenberg School of Communications, and WNET/New York produced the eight-part documentary, *Brain, Mind, and Behavior*, with an accompanying textbook published by W. J. Freeman and Company. Other books explaining brain physiology and cognition were newly available.

One of the earliest pronouncements I can recall was a statement about eighty-five percent of the information we take in each day being visual information. Another statement of like impact was that the brain stores information in visual patterns. I was listening to Dr. Joan Fulton in a summer course at Radford University, and I kept trying to connect my experience with what I was hearing. Twenty-five years ago, however, the basic idea of memory being stored as visual patterns was hard for me to take in at first. But the more I read and listened, the more I realized that I was a visual learner, and I even had visual patterns of my own representing some abstract ideas. How many of my students, with the visual orientation of their own world, were more prone to visual learning than, say, learning from what they heard?

I could easily see that if one heard the word *horse* spoken, each individual might have a different image of a horse in mind. My image was always a brown horse running in a fenced-in meadow, mane blowing in the wind, a slight hill behind him in the background. Who saw mustangs? . . . Pintos? . . . Arabians?

Nouns would understandably produce images of what they were when they were concrete things. Actions/verbs would probably be stored as short mental film-clips, perhaps animated film, in the mind; someone would be running if the verb were *running*. Variations in color, size, and detail would take care of adjectives, and variations in the running action would take care of adverbs. Anyone watching *Sesame Street* with a preschooler knows that the program helps toddlers learn positions of things: over, under, near, beside—prepositions! But abstract ideas were another matter!

It took me a while and a bit of reading about the brain to recall a discussion I had years ago with a colleague on the faculty of a school in the Middle East, when we both discovered that we pictured a year as an ellipse in our minds. His ellipse stretched straight out in front of his mental eyes, and he was standing at the point where the year began, that is, January.

I, for some reason, probably focusing on academic year calendars with an eye toward summer vacation, looked at my elliptical year from the standpoint of spring, with summer to my right, fall in the distance, winter starting just before the farthest point of the ellipse (December reaching into January most likely), before spring arrived again, to my left, to complete the trip.

And did I not remember having to draw pictures to solve story problems in arithmetic and algebra classes? I was definitely a visual learner. I thought that even if a child were an audio or tactile learner, for example, visual strategies would still provide a foundation for taking in, retaining, and retrieving information learned. I realized anew how difficult learning must be for a blind person. Visual information was unavailable except through the other senses.

Of course not all learning is sight based. Everything helped in its own way. We have mnemonic devices for certain content material. When I was growing up, I thought one of the silliest devices I ever heard was the sentence, "George Edward's old grandmother rode a pig home yesterday." Who had to struggle that much to remember how to spell geography?

More recently, Merilee Sprenger (1999) has reported that the two categories of memory established earlier, declarative (facts) and procedural (the how-to's), have been widened to five *memory lanes* as a result of today's advanced technologies. PET scans and MRIs allow researchers to watch the brain's activity in responding to subjects performing different tasks. Sprenger describes these memory pathways as: "semantic, episodic, procedural, automatic, and emotional" (p. 46, 50).

The mid-twentieth-century Hollywood star, Bette Davis, is credited with saying, "Getting old is not for sissies." But as you age, you notice changes in the way your mind works and the way you call on stored-up memories to share, reminisce, or amaze your grandchildren. Researchers have noted that when older people cannot recall something at first try, they approach retrieval from another direction. They cannot think of someone's last name, but if they picture the person in a typical setting with other people known at the same time, invariably the last name pops up as connected with shared friends in that instance.

In another example, a date refuses to identify itself from long-term memory storage. The older person thinks of what was happening and where in the sequence of important experiences the instance occurred or where they were at the time, and they reason out that it was, "the fall of 1963, November, because that was when President Kennedy was assassinated." Some people have suggested, recently, that a new date shared by everyone is 9/11 (September 11th, 2001), when the World Trade Towers were attacked and destroyed in New York City.

Teacher preparation courses emphasize teaching content by involving as many of the senses as possible to ensure stronger storage in memory. Unless sight or hearing impaired, children initially absorb information through the eyes, with the ears providing language terms for what they are seeing, ostensibly for the first time in an academic setting. Visual storage would and should be the basis for each new concept taught, but it must be visual storage that represents the essentials of each new idea. With that statement, something must be mentioned about two related items that are often noted when people are first introduced to visual patterns as part of cognitive instruction: flow charts and graphic organizers.

Early computer programmers developed ways to plot programs that involved *trees and branches* and lots of if/then statements, laying out the intricacies in charts that had connected and interconnected rectangles representing necessary junctures. Programmers moved more easily through the various possibilities with the visual layout. Flow charts were used in classrooms to follow historical events, biological changes in plants or biomes, and so forth.

With graphic organizers, adherents knew that images brought up lots of associated information. Think of the slides shows and photos, souvenirs of a wonderful vacation trip, that we want to share with friends and family. "Here we are on London Bridge. Phew! It was hot for Britain that day. We'd just come from a lunch on a barge restaurant and were headed for the new Globe Theatre."

For teaching purposes, a graphic organizer for a textbook chapter on the history of London in Shakespeare's time could be a teacher's handout showing London Bridge. Some small boats and other craft could be included on the Thames below, and perhaps a glimpse of the Globe Theatre on a far bank. Students would take notes on the scene, filling in pennants and banners and even a cloud or two in the sky. Were the Vikings being studied, a graphic organizer could be a Viking ship with all the shields hanging along the side of the vessel, ready to be filled in with notes, fact phrases more easily recalled once the image of the boat were brought to mind.

A title of a resource available late in the twentieth century was *Visual Tools for Constructing Knowledge* by David Heyerle (1996), published by the Association for Supervision and Curriculum Development (ASCD). Mind-mapping, brainstorming webs, thinking processes, and thinking maps are a few of the topics dealt with in the seven chapters. In fact, the author and colleagues have a website (thinkingmaps.com) where you can see the maps or diagrams they use to teach students patterns of thinking. All can be helpful in the classroom in particular settings.

Brain-based instruction, or cognitive instruction, is organized around visual patterns. They are patterns presented in such a way as to mimic the way a child's mind would see or confront the information in real life. Psychologists, studying the way toddlers learn about their environment even before they can speak about it, have noticed that little ones see only two or three dogs, for example, before they learn the label "dog" or some way of showing that they know the thing is a dog. In most cases, nouns are the first language category to be acquired, followed by verbs. Relationship words come later.

A teaching strategy important to classroom presentations involves showing students examples of the concept from which they can determine defining details or characteristics, the same way they first discerned the differences between dogs and cats. From those traits, they decide on the nature of the concept itself. With enough clear information, students store visual representations more securely than with traditional methods. Given enough information, the memory stored is clear and accurate; if details are insufficient, the brain will fill in the missing parts so the frontal lobes achieve the closure they seem to need. It is a delicate balance for the teacher to give enough information, not too little nor too much.

This book sets out the basics for presenting initial concepts that underpin curriculum in different ways. The chapters will share several patterns the author has found essential in her classroom experiences: ABLGUF (a nickname for a complete description pattern, pronounced able-goof), a paragraph, outlines, the culture box, the event-frame in its various modifications, a basic map, time line, and visual symbols for English grammar, namely the basic eight parts of speech and sentence structure.

Hang on. Here we go!

●

BRAIN PROCESSES
FOR LEARNING AND MEMORY
AND HOW YOU CAN HELP

The whole art of teaching is only the art of awakening the natural curiosity of young minds for the purpose of satisfying it afterwards.

—Anatole France, novelist, essayist, Nobel laureate (1844–1924)

It will not require hypnotism, sodium pentothal, or lots of sessions on a psychiatrist's couch retrieving buried memories; once you begin thinking about how the mind thinks, you will start thinking about how you think, and then you will remember instances that match with your experiences, and you will be hooked.

Have you lived long enough to raise a couple of children of your own? Did you ever baby-sit with infants or preschoolers? Did you have younger siblings you helped with as they grew up? Have you realized that you have some lasting memories that come from very early in your life, even though they say we remember little if anything specific from before the age of four? You have personal experience to bring to the discussion of how the brain, the mind, learns new things and remembers them, with or without parents, teachers, or coaches. We are wired for learning—learning from experience from our own personal *day one*.

Newborn infants, starting their first month of life, learn to recognize their mothers' faces. There have been programs on public television about research with infants of six months to toddler-age that show they respond to their mothers' faces differently, depending on whether the mother looks happy or sad and upset. The brain is organized to recognize things, which means it can sort through what it has seen before and compare it to what it is seeing at the moment. That was a survival skill for prehistoric humans: recognize the familiar and be afraid of the unfamiliar that might turn out to be dangerous, even fatal.

For young babies to recognize their mothers and how their mothers are feeling, they have to know what faces are, and that means they have to notice and recognize "eyes, ears, mouth, and nose," as the song goes. We spend our lives analyzing or taking apart things that we see so we can remember and decide what they are when they show up in our sphere again some day.

Youngsters spend the first five years of their lives learning the language and what they will probably see in their environments—friends, other adults than parents, workers, buildings, animals, plants, household contents, clothing—the list is endless. Parents teach them new words, check them when reading picture books ("What do we call this animal?" and "What does the pig say?"), and provide as many experiences as they can as a background for future learning.

My principal in an elementary school in Nashville, Tennessee, once announced casually that he had to take his two children to a farm. They could not tell the difference between a cow and a horse, he explained. Children do not have trouble telling the difference between cats and dogs at an early age and after having seen only a few household pets; but, pictures in books about farm animals probably do not have enough of the defining atmosphere on a two-dimensional page and might take a little more first-hand experience. The labeling process continues for all of life, and the information gained is stored in growing brains, as well as mature ones, to help distinguish things as horizons expand.

I liked the way the authors of *A Perfect Mess,* Eric Abrahamson and David H. Freedman, described children's language acquisition in a chapter called "Messy Thinking." Here is a bit of redundancy for your entertainment:

> As almost any parent can attest, a five-month-old infant need only run into
> two or three dogs before he has formulated a mental category for them to

store alongside the categories of caregivers, strangers, food, and toys. At first, dogs might be lumped in with all animals in the infant's mind, but soon dogs, cats, squirrels, and other intriguing creatures are all given their own subcategories. We are literally born categorizers and for good reason; there isn't enough time when we encounter each new entity in the world to go through the process of carefully observing and analyzing it so that we can finally decide if we need to pet it, eat it, flee from it, or smile at it. How much more efficient to quickly determine what easily flagged characteristics certain entities have in common, come up with some useful generalizations about this group of entities, and then apply those generalizations to every new entity that seems to fit . . . " (2006, p. 257)

Most of what infants, toddlers, and preschoolers learn are things they see and hear and things they do with caregivers, parents, or siblings. An initial experience—seeing a bird on a tree branch, petting a neighbor's dog—is repeated over time and becomes familiar, stored as a generalization, a prototype. Learning is incidental and long-lasting, too. As early as 1982, Donald Norman stated: "My belief is that visual memory serves the later stages of processing by maintaining an image for a sufficient length of time to let those stages do their jobs" (p. 9). Dr. Jay Geidd asserts, "The human brain is still the best at pattern recognition" (Wallis, 2004, p. 59).

Young children learn from positive and negative experiences, and sometimes the emotional overlay makes the memory much stronger than one would expect. Think of seeing the witch on her broomstick flying in the film *The Wizard of Oz*. Do you still remember how you reacted? I do. In a recent issue of *Time* magazine, Michael D. Lemonick quotes James McGaugh, a neurobiologist at the University of California at Irvine, as saying, "Any kind of emotional experience will create a stronger memory than otherwise would be created . . . The major purpose of memory is to predict the future" (2007, p. 103).

But at the same time that they are building a vocabulary, preschoolers are learning where they go with their families and what they do in certain situations—fast-food franchises or sit-down restaurants with waiters, meetings, or play dates. Head Start, preschools, or kindergartens introduce them to routines such as careful handling of scissors and a myriad of topics and materials. Early childhood in the television era includes special programming for youngsters on television, videos, and DVDs. Unless something is wrong from the start, the children cannot help but learn. We know the truism: they absorb what they see and hear like sponges.

As research into child development and brain development has added to our knowledge about learning and memory, companies have started or built on established reputations to produce educational toys marked for the appropriate ages. They acquaint children with colors, letters, numbers, counting, telling time, building with blocks, and playing with child-sized versions of kitchens—playing out what they see their parents doing. The selection seems infinite and the variety amazing. Having learned those things to which children respond, designers and manufacturers of the toys make sure they are full of bright colors, sounds, music, and often flashing lights. If future interior designers combine purple with chartreuse and pink, we will understand why.

In some ways, how a child learns and remembers is something we have observed for generations and have come to expect, according to plotted developmental timetables. Brain research is using CAT scans and magnetic resonance imaging (MRI) to observe electrical activity in the brain and adding to those observations. Scientists note where the activity is located in response to the type of stimuli they present. Their findings are compared to research on adult brains that has allowed us to map brain regions.

Researchers have mapped areas for verbal language, emotional centers, factual memory storage, short-term memory (even down to where nouns seem to be stored), and noted the active thinking and reasoning locations in the frontal lobes. It is this information on which classroom teachers can build and plan their instruction. They can teach with strategies that imitate the way the infant, toddler, and preschool brains take in and store the knowledge they bring to what they call real or regular school.

Good classrooms and exceptional schools provide wide experiences that include physical activity, variety, and even novelty during a school day. Research has shown that the brain is attracted to new things, colorful things, closed shapes (as opposed to pages of print or handwritten script), and things that appear complete and do not lack so much information as to be confusing. Eric Jensen states, "If the novelty is strong enough, the likely recall of the material goes up dramatically" (1998, p. 106). Little children put labels on things they have seen or experienced. Older children continue to learn labels for things and ideas, even abstractions, and they acquire physical skills in reading, sports, music, artistic techniques, and academic learning. How *do* classroom teachers present academic content in a way that is compatible with brain processes?

A teacher might prepare for a particular new topic by asking some questions:

1. What exactly is it that I want the students to remember?
2. What does this look like (a challenge for ideas versus things)?
3. What are the parts of the whole that children need to know to understand the complete thing or concept?
4. What would be some appropriate examples to show the class?
5. How can I present the examples for students to scrutinize?
6. What details should I be sure they see and take note of?
7. What visual representation will I present to them, and how will it be labeled?
8. What other examples might I expect the students to suggest?

Visual representations for concepts to store in the mind are much like foundational support. They might be confused with the term *scaffolding*, situations in which the teacher provides enough structure for an activity, a lesson, or project so the student has sufficient information to do the assignment, even though the child might not have all the background needed at that moment. As the child matures, less and less scaffolding is needed as they work toward independence.

Morton Hunt addresses mental images in *The Universe Within*: "Thinking in imagery may well have come before thinking in words . . . but what kind of images were they and what kind of thinking was it? Probably extremely simple and, like the thinking of a preverbal child, limited to the physical here and now. Advanced thinking depends on the mental manipulation of symbols" (1982, p. 227).

Irvine Sigel's studies help us understand concept construction. He based his work on the relationship between the representations that children store in their minds and their ability to distance themselves from the present to remember something from previous experience. In an article about Sigel's work, the authors Ellsworth and Sindt, explain that "mental activities such as images or words . . . stand for something. Everything we know is represented mentally in some form or another" (1994, pp. 40–41).

Visual representations work in a similar fashion as scaffolding when a child learns a concept and then refers to it in memory on a future occasion. A child that was taught with the visual patterns approach will bring up the mental image of, for example, a paragraph—a rectangle with the corner cut out—and that will help her remember the verbal information attached to that image, such as an introduction, a main idea, supporting sentences, and some type of ending statement. When assigned an essay or a simple paragraph to write, the students will recall instinctively the image of the paragraph shape and visualize the parts and language labels as they get involved in doing the assignment. These visual patterns, however, represent the concept itself.

Classroom teachers and those who work with children on a regular basis occasionally question the emphasis on visual storage in the brain and on teaching in a way that focuses on visual information. They usually ask, "What about the auditory learner?" (No one has ever asked me about the kinesthetic learner.) But research has shown that memory for the average student is created of visual information. If a concept is introduced in a classroom with examples, no matter what they are—they might be examples of paintings, songs, stories, arithmetic exercises, and such—all will be seen or heard, discussed, analyzed to find commonalities, and then a way of recording the shared traits will be devised by the group or presented by the teacher.

Musical notation is a visual representation of heard melody lines, but for students not yet acquainted with notes and the musical staff, an actual line might be drawn, rising and falling by degrees relative to the tune. Besides, the more the teacher and her students work with the new concepts, the more they will be using other senses, certainly the auditory and kinesthetic.

If a teacher uses visual patterns for concept models as a basic element of teaching, the teacher will accumulate either a lot of posters to store, a lot of overhead transparencies, or many computer-scanned and stored files that can be projected in the classroom efficiently, perhaps on an interactive white board (a white board with electronic note-taking capabilities) connected to a computer and projector. I have searched for the term "multimedia projectors" online and discovered they can project any visual material that your computer can handle: CD, DVD, and graphics files. There is also a contemporary version of an old warhorse, the opaque projector. Elmo manufactures a number of visual presenters and the electronic imaging projector. You can put various materials, such as a three-dimensional object, papers, or open books, on these projectors and then choose the size to project for your class.

As long as there have been blackboards and slates, teachers have drawn pictures and labeled them to help students understand information and solve problems. In ancient cultures, they drew in the sand with sticks. Modern technology will, perhaps, ease the teaching process along, but brain research will be right behind it to give it authority.

2

THE VALUE OF A COMPLETE DESCRIPTION: ABLGUF

Verbal descriptions are essential in everyday living, general conversation, and certainly the workplace. Imagine giving directions to a driver without adding more detail than just right or left, mileage, and the compass directions! How could teenagers describe the new-found objects of their passing affections? Where would the fashion industry and the advertising world be without the language skills to describe the product and tempt the buyer? We cannot function without the skill to describe what we mean, but we all know people who give vague descriptions that require questioning them for more information.

Dr. Joan Fulton (1986) designed a visual concept-model for what she called the "six dimensions of a complete description," which appealed strongly to young children. She would display a picture of "Harold, the Monster," which had been constructed from a horse's seemingly transparent body—but you didn't see internal organs—with *three* pairs of chicken legs, a geometric mane, and a ridiculous face. Harold had exaggerated nostrils like a startled dinosaur in a comic book, a horn like a rhinoceros, and a swirling tail that was both geometric and reptilian.

Once seen, Harold was hard to forget. And radiating out from Harold, going before him, were the six dimensions needed to completely describe most anything, clearly numbered, and having additional details:

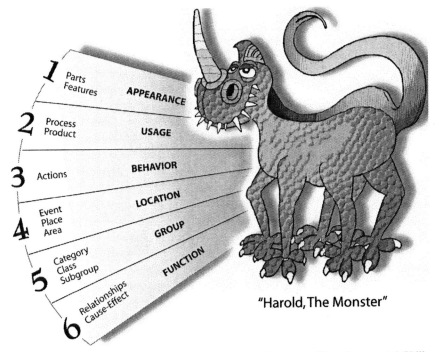

Figure 2.1a.   Six ways to describe: Harold, the Monster (Developmental Skills Institute)

1. Appearance—parts and features
2. Behavior—actions
3. Location—event, time, place, area
4. Group—category, class, subgroup
5. Usage—process and product
6. Function—relationships, cause and effect

Harold has matured since his first manifestation as described here. You might say he has more substance in this new appearance as shown in figure 2.1a and 2.1b.

Since the majority of my teaching career was spent in middle school classrooms, except for some primary grade substituting and college teacher-training overseas, I wanted a more sophisticated representation of a complete description. I was not, however, above showing the students Harold for his humorous aspects, and for his value in analysis. I used old technology. If you have new machines available, use them.

HAROLD

Figure 2.1.b.   Harold, alone

I would display a transparency of Harold himself, unlabeled. "What have we here?" would be the opening question. And the word *monster* would jump out. "But is he really a monster? Is he scary?" And then the students would begin to focus. They would spot the familiar—the horse-type body, the chicken legs, what looks like a horse's mane but seems to be a solid protuberance—and then someone would say, "He has six—or three pairs of—legs!"

Then the fun begins, because a teacher can ask where students might see one of these monsters, and ask whether they would be frightened and run, or stick around for laughs. Usually someone would say Harold would be in a story or an animated film, which lets the teacher ask what he would do in such a setting and what colors would the animators give him. And is this a small monster and friendly, or a huge one and scary due to his size? Harold was a very useful introduction for preteens who still had the enthusiasms of childhood with more mature thinking and reasoning skills. They would enter into the fun. Adapt him to the high-school level by suggesting students plan an animated film starring Harold, and go from there.

Sooner or later, we would get around to the concept of the complete description as opposed to a vague description or a partial description. For example, we would discuss why incomplete descriptions might lead to social or communication problems.

The visual representation of the six dimensions of a description that I decided to use came from basic common fractions and the idea of the whole being the sum of the parts. A circle divided equally into sixths served to show the elements and their composite *whole*. I was even guilty of color-coding the sixths as pie-shaped pieces and manipulating them to build a whole circle on the bulletin board, magnetic blackboard, or overhead transparency. Appearance was red, Behavior was green, Location might have been a lighter shade of green, and Group was definitely blue. I probably kept the lighter shade of green for Usage and Functions, as outgrowths of actions or behaviors. The ultimate circle-whole (shown in figure 2.2), with the six sixths composing it, was always labeled on the outer rim with the names of the various dimensions.

I put the six dimensions in order beginning with Appearance because that is the aspect you note first when you see something. Appearance is followed by Behavior (or actions), since one notices what something is doing after the initial spotting. And then comes Location, where this thing is seen doing what it does. After that is Group, because by then, unless it were an alien or unknown plant or animal, most things seen have categories into which they can be filed mentally. The final two dimensions—Usage and Function—were a little trickier in describing anything. We will get to them later.

When a math-science teacher, with whom I was teamed at the time, wanted to use some of the visual representations in teaching his subject areas, he found he had trouble remembering the six parts. He would come over to my classroom area, around the dividing screen in our

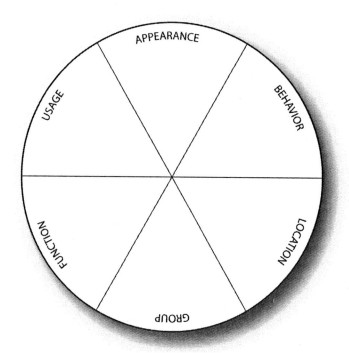

Figure 2.2.   **Six dimensions, blank—circle of sixths, labeled**

open-space classrooms, and check out the circle labels on the posted pattern. It was he who came up with the nickname, "able-goof," by picking up the beginning letters of each dimension and reversing the Usage and Function labels from the charted sequence in order to create something pronounceable, but silly enough to be memorable:

A for Appearance
B for Behavior
L for Location
G for Group
U for Usage
F for Function

And that spells "ABLGUF" (able-goof).

I liked this order for the seeming logic of it. As mentioned above, you saw something, how it appeared to you, and then watched how it behaved, what it did. You saw the setting in which it appeared and categorized it as to how you would group it with other similar things. Then came its use: whatever it was, acting as it did, produced something, even if it were only to sit there and look attractive, like a Chinese vase from the Ming Dynasty sitting on a shelf in a tastefully decorated home. The process of sitting produced or contributed to its attractive environment, and thus it *functioned* in that environment—it made it attractive and elicited comments from appreciative visitors.

Students usually understand the function of a messy bedroom and its effect on their parents better than Ming vases, however.

ABLGUF proved to be handy in many situations. In fact, I would tell my middle school students that they would use it all their lives: they could write love letters describing themselves as worthy of the other person's affections, or they could describe a house if they went into the real estate business. And those were just two adult situations. In the classroom, once introduced, it could be used orally in class discussions: think of show and tell and sharing times in kindergarten and primary grades, with a large chart displaying *Harold* or ABLGUF nearby, and teacher or students referring to that chart when sharing information.

It could be used in oral storytelling and reporting. It was a map or outline that could be employed differently depending on the students. Children just beginning to write their own reports and stories might produce a single summary paragraph with a sentence for each aspect of the description. It guided note-taking. When ready to do initial research online or in the school library, or in writing up what they had learned about something in science or social studies, each dimension could become a paragraph in itself. With a good deal of information for a report on an extinct species, for example, or one seemingly doomed to extinction in our modern world, each element might be dealt with thoroughly in more than one paragraph.

WAYS TO INTRODUCE A COMPLETE DESCRIPTION

You can do no better than to introduce ABLGUF right at the beginning of a school year. Everyone is relatively new to each other—new teachers, some new classmates most likely, or some complete newcomers to town or the neighborhood. Everyone will be in a situation where there is a need to get to know someone. We tell children not to judge a book by its cover, and yet we know when we meet a new person, the *cover* is the first thing we see. How we react to the appearance of a person new to us colors how we will respond to the rest of the individual, his or her personality, as it unfolds. The remainder of the chapter will show some examples of how to introduce ABLGUF.

Getting to Know You (as in the song from The King and I)

Teachers usually have a certain amount of *ham* in them; they can act out various parts or roles as needed. One way to demonstrate an example of ABLGUF is to talk about all the new people we meet at the beginning of school. Sometimes, even after the school year has started, the principal will come to the classroom door with a new pupil who has just arrived to join the class group. The teacher can ask the class how they would react to a student who comes in with the principal and first is introduced to the teacher. How would they react if the student waited, stood looking at the floor the whole time, perhaps twisting part of an article of clothing? The teacher would act out this behavior to demonstrate.

Or, what if the student stood with one hip cocked out, and an arm bent akimbo, hand on hip, staring unblinkingly at the rest of the class, almost in defiance, certainly with bravado? How would the students decide if they wanted to go up to either of these students at lunchtime and try to make friends? Appearance and behavior are going to be definite influences in this case. But do not forget to end this lesson with, "You can't judge a book by its cover."

In the twenty-first century, teachers cannot count on students of any age recognizing the song "Getting to Know You," from the Broadway musical *The King and I* (Rogers and Hammerstein, 1951); but, they can allude to a Broadway show with older students anyway. Tell them it was a show that had a woman who went to teach the children of a king in a country that is now called Thailand, and she sang a song that went . . . (and that is the cue to sing a bit in performance if you have an average voice, a good sense of pitch, and self-confidence). And you do not have to sing for long. Otherwise, you can just make the allusion and introduce some questions that would help.

"There you are, in the cafeteria, or with your lunchbox at a table in the classroom, or somewhere in between." Depending on the student's age and maturity level, he or she might smile and ask the newcomer:

"Where are you from?" "Where do you live in town?" (location)
"What do you like to do?" (behavior)
"Do you play sports?" (usage = process and product)
"Do you want to be a cheerleader?" (or a pitcher?)

The student might think,

"Will you be better at it than I am?" (function—relationship, cause/effect)
"What are you interested in?"
"Do you have any hobbies? Any pastimes?" (usage again)
"Do you have any brothers or sisters?"
". . . any other family members living with you?" (group)
"I'm Irish. Where's your family from?" (group)
"I'm so glad to find someone else with freckles!" (appearance)

Interviewing a Classmate to Introduce that Student

If there is time for interaction and students are mature enough to handle it, you might have students interview each other and get a *complete description* of a class member before introducing them to the rest of the group in their turn.

Sometimes a distinction between Usage (what can you actually do?) and Function (in the environment) is needed. Keep emphasizing the process and product idea for Usage, and the setting or environment, in which the thing produced relates to its setting, for Function—cause and effect. How do you use this thing? What does it produce? What is the result wherever it is?

Just ask what happens when one of the students' habits at home produces a messy bedroom or playroom, as mentioned above. Students can see that it was their process of turning their bedrooms or playrooms into a mess (the product) that affected their mother in such a way that, as part of their environment, she gave them an ultimatum for picking up the room in no uncertain terms. Students do not usually think about how they affect their environment, but you need not push this one too hard.

For this class activity, you can hand out copies of a blank circle divided into sixths, and have the students label each sixth outside the section and take notes about their classmates inside the circle.

What on Earth Is This?

For younger children, illustrations of animals in their habitats, pro-
gressively displayed in what might be called *layers,* is quite effective,
and works well with all ages. I have traced or sketched outlines of selected animals with very little detail, just outlines that included body,
limbs, and head with eyes and mouth. For our thinking here, let us consider what looks like a lizard, as seen in figures 2.3 through 2.6. The animal can be presented with a series of transparencies prepared ahead,
with the first outline used as the foundation and the rest as additional
overlays. A set of PowerPoint slides works well, too. If the teacher has
artistic skill and drawing speed, the animal can be presented as a chalk-
talk, making the initial sketch and adding textures and details as the
scene moves toward being complete.

If you need to pinch pennies, you can prepare two cut-outs of the animal in outline, but the second cutout would have colored-in details to
show, for example, the texture or pattern on the reptile's skin. Glue a
piece of flannel on the back of each prepared piece and use them on a
flannel board or pin them to the bulletin board.

With this first bare outline, simply ask what it is, and then ask, "Are
you sure?" Put enough inflection in that second question to suggest perhaps they are not quite right and need to think some more. Sound really

What is this?

Are you sure?

Figure 2.3.   Goanna in silhouette

Do you need more information?

Figure 2.4.   Goanna with scales—texture

confused at their answer. It makes them think again, even if they were right the first time. Chances are, to the lizard-like outline, you will hear students say, "A lizard," "A chameleon," or even "A Gila monster!"

Place a second transparency over the first, or put the second colored and patterned reptile on the flannel board, or quickly chalk-in some suggested

Does this help any?

Why?

Figure 2.5.   Goanna environment—rocks and grasses

Figure 2.6. Complete goanna scene

patterning on the animal's outline and ask, "Do you need more information?"

Or you might ask, "What don't you know at this point?" Change your questioning to suit the age group with which you are working. Draw some grassy clumps and rocks around the chalked lizard-shape, or place flannel-backed vegetation and rocks around the posted lizard, or put yet another transparency atop the first with the clumps of grass and groupings of rocks in place. Or just show the rocks and tussocks of grass.

If you are using transparencies, the three, layered this way, produce the final scene (see figure 2.6).

Ask, again, if they need more information. (They do not know how tall the grasses are or how large the rocks are to gauge the size of the *lizard*.)

Next show a map of Australia (as in figure 2.7) or wherever this representative reptile is found in nature. Ask, "Where are we?"

And if you cannot use an Australian animal or something too exotic with your youngest students, choose accordingly. The only thing to keep in mind is to choose an animal that could be easily misidentified because of a common-looking outline. A species of barnyard fowl would work

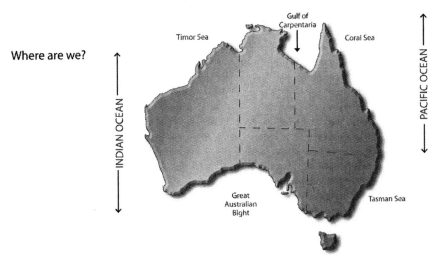

Figure 2.7.   Outline map of Australia

well, or a common wild bird. Considering the variety of squirrels—gray, red, black, flying—they might be a good bet, too.

Guide the class in rethinking. Tell them, "Think back."

1. What did you see first?
2. What information was added?
3. How did seeing the rocks, sand, and clumps of grass (tussocks) help?
4. Did you ever know what to call this?
5. How did the map help?
6. Is there something left that you still don't know? (relative size)

At this point you can display a descriptive paragraph for students who can read well, who already read to find out information. Again, on a transparency, you can highlight in color the parts of the text that have words to describe the appearance of the reptile, where it lives, what it does, etc. In this situation, used regularly with incoming sixth graders, I projected the following paragraph:

Goanna

Goannas are large lizards like the monitor lizards of other countries. Australia has many varieties of goanna, varying in length from about one foot up to eight feet. A goanna's skin is covered with small oval scales, which look like chain mail. Its tongue is long, purple or black in color and forked like the tongue of a snake. Most goannas are expert climbers and have long, curved claws. These help them both in climbing trees and in foraging for their food, which consists mainly of insects, carrion, small birds and animals, and sometimes other lizards or even snakes. Most goannas are also splendid runners. They run fastest on four legs, but in high grass or scrub, they sometimes stand up and run on their hind legs, only so that they can keep an eye on their pursuers. The Perenty Goanna is the largest one found in Australia. It lives in dry, desert areas where it makes its home by burrowing under rocks. Like other goannas, it lays eggs from which the young are produced.

Children's specialized coloring books like those published by the Dover Press—my son had one on sharks—can be helpful. Science teacher colleagues usually have materials ready for display with suitable information that would be an example of a "complete description." The Perenty Goanna information above came from a coloring book from the Australian Embassy in Beirut, Lebanon, some years ago, *Your Colouring Book of Australian Birds and Animals.*

At this point, the students have a concept of a description and what it should include to be clear and definite. They should have a copy of the pattern, or visual representation, labeled with the six dimensions as seen in figure 2.8. For young children, a poster the teacher can bring out during discussion or writing time will suffice. But it helps not to stop here. Practice recognizing good descriptions in subsequent lessons on this topic or related ones until ABLGUF is a *done deal.*

Practice Activities to Ensure Storage of Pattern

You can play a guessing game by making sets of six cards, each having a dimension of a description of a chosen animal. Prepare sets of cards for at least three animals, or if you prefer, objects students meet regularly in daily life. Or prepare enough sets of six cards per *thing* so that each person in the class can be given a single card. To play the game, distribute the cards. Have students take turns reading one card at a time. If another student thinks he has another part of the same description, he raises a hand and is called on to share. The object is to

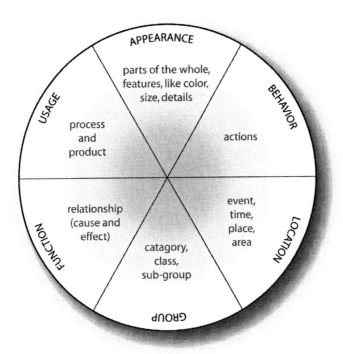

Figure 2.8.   ABLGUF circle labeled with details

complete a description and identify the animal or thing; the student who does, wins.

If you have access to an overhead projector, select three objects or things to describe. Type up and print out three pages, each with six paragraphs, one for each of the dimensions of a description but does not actually name the things being described. Make each sheet into a transparency that you can cut apart and manipulate on the overhead projector.

You might have something, such as shown in figure 2.9, on one sheet to make your transparency and then it cut apart into six "see-through cards."

Prepare three sets of see-through cards from transparencies for three quadrupeds, but with enough distinctions to allow students to recognize them as three different animals. For my sixth graders, a tiger, a moose or elk, and a llama (described in the card set) had enough in common, but were distinctive enough to spur thinking and interest.

For this game, put the three Appearance dimension cards on the overhead projector and have the students read them. Then start adding

Llama Cards

BEHAVIOR: I can trot, walk, and run. I nibble grass and other grains. I'm at my best in cool, high altitudes, otherwise, I droop.	APPEARANCE: I have a small head with two perky ears on a long neck. My rather large body is covered with long, silky hair and held up by four skinny legs. My feet are hooves.
GROUP: I'm a quadruped, a four-footed animal. Actually I'm related to a camel, but we are not on the same continent.	LOCATION: You'll find me in the mountains of South America, a very useful beast.
FUNCTION: I carry heavy loads on my back, up and down the Andes Mountains.	USAGE: My strong back and sure-footed sharp hooves make me a great pack animal, but my long fur spins into wonderful, soft, warm wool.

Figure 2.9. Llama cards

other cards and have the class decide under which animal's description the additional cards should go. Somewhere along the line, students will begin to decide they are ready to guess. It is okay to let them guess—right or wrong, you can continue the game until all aspects are lined up under the various animals correctly or a wrong guess is corrected with further information. It is never too early to show students that information is fluid, and what we know changes as new knowledge is available.

Small groups of students could collaborate, producing sets of six cards with which to challenge another group or the class as a whole.

Version Two of the Guessing Game

Another approach is to start with any see-through card and begin grouping the cards as they accumulate and students see relationships. The ages of your students will determine the most effective approach. If you start with the three appearance cards the first time, you can use a random approach another time to be more of a challenge.

The Budget Version of the Guessing Game

Depending on the equipment to which you have access, you might play this game and produce a bulletin board for which you really should be ready to add the animals' pictures at the end. Use a word processor and type the various cards in a very large font size that would be readable by the class sitting at their desks, or the group could be brought to the bulletin board area where they might see better sitting on the carpet.

You could have the large-print cards read aloud and posted where the students think they fit, or you could have them scrambled on the bulletin board to rearrange in the right columns, perhaps under those attractive pictures of said animals. "Where there's a will, there's a way," even around the most stringent budget in a school system. Contemporary options for projecting materials might adapt to this card-sorting strategy, too.

Guess Who! Paragraphs—or—Guess What! Paragraphs

Another practice with the idea of a complete description is to write *Guess Who?* or *Guess What?* paragraphs, depending on the skill level of the students. If the description is complete enough—there *is* room for unintended omissions as the students work on their own—students can read their paragraphs and merely have classmates guess the thing being described. They can even read them sentence by sentence, and classmates can decide which aspect of a description (ABLGUF) is being shared.

Remember ABLGUF when teaching adjectives during a grammar lesson. Students can illustrate anything from Hallowe'en witches to famous Americans (like Daniel Boone or Abraham Lincoln; avoid celebrities) and write an accompanying descriptive paragraph. With the pictures posted on the bulletin board, the students read their paragraphs, and the class tries to match them. If the description is not complete or details in the picture are omitted in the paragraph, not only do they see that adjectives are important, but so is detail.

By *using* the circle-pattern of a complete description to process student information, you will find it *functions* in several classroom environments.

Show-and-Tell in kindergarten and early grades will be a natural situation in which to help children remember to describe completely the item they have brought to school. In science classes, where topics for note-taking and reporting are legion, the six dimensions can be a checklist to see if the necessary information was included in the report. Social studies is another area where note-taking and reporting, discussing historic leaders, places, or things, can benefit from a student's use of the complete description pattern. To reiterate its support in actual writing assignments, a short paragraph can summarize the topic by touching on all six dimensions or ways to describe. But if each dimension is well developed, perhaps in a paragraph of its own or multiple paragraphs, an extensive, thorough report is the result.

Teachers and parents can extend students' critical thinking skills by focusing on the complete description pattern. In a situation where something is confusing, questions can be based on the dimensions. What do we need to know more of here? What information is missing? Do the conclusions reached come logically from how this topic operates in society? Did this invention cause the effects in the industrial world that the inventor expected?

Refer to these six dimensions frequently, using them in your verbal and written directions, and in reminding students when the description pattern will be helpful in various assignments and class activities. Use a large, posted pattern of the circle in sixths to reinforce the idea of six parts making a whole. You will find this pattern can help strengthen learning in several areas and subjects.

3

THE INFINITELY FLEXIBLE EVENT FRAME

*E*vent, what a wonderful word! People advertise festivities open to the public as big events, or private parties as private events. "That was a big event in my life," someone will say, reminiscing. Awaiting these events can be nerve wracking, but they happen *eventually*. In using the word, *event*, in this chapter, we will be applying two particular terms from cognitive psychology, from learning and memory research.

Researchers speak of declarative knowledge, the first term, as stored memory in the form of discreet information or facts. We store much more than discreet facts. And we all know how uncomfortable we feel in strange situations, situations we have not been in before and do not know what the correct behavior—the protocol—might be.

One anecdote with which my generation grew up was about tea time at the White House when a visiting Asian dignitary observed a former President pouring some of his tea into his saucer. The occasion must have been somewhat informal, considering it was upstairs in what is actually the President's home. The dignitary followed suit before he noticed the President putting the saucer on the floor for the White House pet. What the dignitary did to get out of his situation was left to the imagination. When folks write in to ask a manners' expert about deportment before an impending big event in their lives, they are told, "Follow your host or hostess's lead." It is an admonition, which, on most occasions, works well.

We might not use the word, *protocol,* as they do in diplomatic circles, but we often ask, "What's the procedure here?" if we feel comfortable doing so in that situation. Stored knowledge about routines, how things are done, how to proceed in certain settings, is aptly called *procedural knowledge.* That is the second term. Procedural knowledge has been generalized from several similar experiences and stored as *schema.*

As mentioned in the introduction, Merilee Sprenger (1999) reported that these two categories of memory established earlier, declarative (facts) and procedural (the how-to's), now extend to five *memory lanes* due to current technologies. PET scans and MRIs allow researchers to watch the brain's activity as subjects perform various tasks. Sprenger identifies the pathways as—"semantic, episodic, procedural, automatic, and emotional" (pp. 46, 50). The text in this book will mostly refer to the two categories of memory (declarative and procedural information).

Other terms that cognitive psychologists speak of include frames, scripts, and the aforementioned schema. Schemas are routines where knowledge about how to do something is organized along what we might think of as a story script, a series of actions, or frames. This scripted knowledge, of a situation like eating in a restaurant, is stored as procedural knowledge. You can remember the word, *scheme* (a concocted plan to do something), as a memory aid for *schema.* And remember procedural knowledge as all information associated with how to proceed with something. Framing the script or steps for any process means sequencing what needs to be done.

Researchers Donald Norman (1982) and David Rummelhart were sharing their findings in this area when I was first introduced to cognitive instruction. They used the terms *events, frames,* and *schema,* and also *semantic networks*—related vocabulary involved in certain concepts.

One of my stored schemas is how to use a sewing machine, namely mine. Actually I had not used it for several years, as the last decade of my teaching career was extremely hectic, or so it seemed. When I got out the machine for a major project of mending, for a moment I could not remember how to thread it! I could not believe my mental blank. What saved the day was *muscle memory.* I simply started to thread the machine, and the habit of moving my hands with the thread took over and reminded me of what I had momentarily forgotten.

In presenting events and event frames to students, teachers will find that magazines and calendars can afford good photographs of something that is *happening*. I was very fond of a picture of a father obviously helping his young son build a doghouse for the new puppy. With a picture like that, you can ask, "If you were writing a story about this picture, what would the title be?" Or you could ask, "What would you call it?" You could almost win a bet by telling your gambling buddy that someone in the class would call out, "Building a Dog House." It is that certain.

Teachers have used pictures as motivators, or ideas, for story-writing for years and years. Pick the pictures carefully, and you can introduce the abstract idea of an event. And, not to belabor the point, but obviously you can take this further and ask for the steps or actions the characters probably would do in this story—deciding on the doghouse plan, going to shop for materials, measuring carefully, and so forth. You are well on the way to the goal of what a story event frame is and how it works.

I tell students an event frame is an empty comic strip. It is a series of connected boxes that can hold pictures or text and represent an event: fictional events, historical events, and even steps in routines or procedures. As part of cognitive instruction, I learned about organizing and analyzing story plots and character development in *fiction event frames*. These frames can focus on the main actions of a single character, as well as for two or more characters who interact in a plot. We will deal with fiction event frames here, and what we discuss will translate easily to the real or *historic event frame*. Keep that empty comic strip in your mind, but think in terms of the comic strips we see in weekly papers rather than the Sunday *funnies*. Keep an image of three boxes, or even four or five; that is enough for a start.

Back in my childhood and for a few decades more, there was a comic strip called *Henry*. *Henry* did not speak. He would be au courant in some places these days, because he was a young boy and totally bald. If that comic strip were available today, you would have a good source for introducing the concept of story event frames. Use computer graphics to help, if you feel secure with those options. By now, you know I lived with the overhead projector. It was a happy experience in cohabitation.

I hope it would not infringe on copyright laws to make two transparencies or large colored photocopies of a comic strip without speech balloons. Reserve one in entirety and cut the other into the individual frames to manipulate on the overhead projector or on a bulletin board. You can even laminate them and use clothespins (they still make them) to hang them, according to student discussion, in sequence on a wire stretched above the chalkboard. The new-age projectors should work here too.

It is a good challenge for students to interpret pictures without language clues. It strengthens comprehension skills, as well as having youngsters consider the time sequence in which the event developed.

STORY EVENT FRAMES

In kindergarten, and even preschool, teachers use stories with children and discuss them as an essential part of language development, to say nothing of thinking in terms of events and the people involved. Usually the teachers tell children that stories have a beginning, a middle, and an end. That is where the three-box comic strip, as shown in figure 3.1, comes in.

Teachers can prepare transparencies for various story event frames so they are ready to write on with water-based markers. Those notes can be wiped away to clean the transparency for the next time. New or renovated schools may have classrooms with ceiling-mounted projectors connected to both video-streaming cable and the classroom computers. They project onto an interactive white board as mentioned in chapter one, that connects electronically back to the teacher's computer. Scanning an event frame pattern to project on the white board should be easy for the technologically coordinated.

For kindergarten and early primary classes, reproducing a blank event frame on poster board and laminating it so you can write on it, as the discussion proceeds, is an efficient way to be ready for anything resembling *the teachable moment*. Just grab the white-board markers and run. Clean up afterwards or keep for reviewing.

The glory of the event frame stems from the clear visual messages it sends. The boxes move from left to right the same way we read English text; the boxes in sequence remind us of wall calendars, as time moves through the week being represented. Often what happens on Monday affects what happens on Tuesday, or there is a series of things that have to be done over two or three days, so the event frame suggests sequence, and also cause and effect.

A story has three parts:

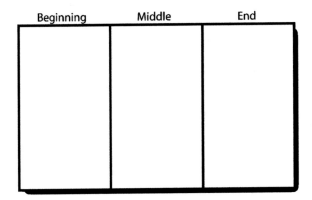

Beginning	Middle	End

Decide on these elements:

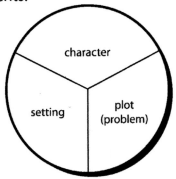

character

setting

plot (problem)

You can change them for new story events!

Figure 3.1. Beginning event frame—three-frames, story circle

How to Use It: From Folk Tales to Shakespeare

In discussing a story read to or read with the class, the group identifies the main character and then the main character's most important actions. Most students will locate actions in general and have to be led to see what a main action is. Yawning or making a face at an annoying sibling is not important and certainly not a main action. The main actions move the story plot along. The teacher can ask what the character *did*

and jot down on the side of the event frame the actions the children suggest. "Which ones are most important?" Then it is time to ask, "Which
action did Susie do first?" That initial action is written in the first frame
on the transparency, wipe-off poster, or white board. And the story
analysis continues from there.

With kindergartners, where the three-part story's beginning, middle,
and end are the focus, sequencing is no problem; it is too obvious. As
the main character is more active, so to say, sequencing the actions may
raise debate, as you will see in figure 3.2. Teachers should always ask
why the character did what he or she did, bringing out a bit of character development appropriate to maturity of the students, but also the
idea of one thing leading to another. Because the character was in this
situation, it seemed wise to do the action he or she did; but why did the
character do the next action? Action and reaction become the order of
the day, with character intentions or goals a parallel topic.

Teachers write the name of the action or a phrase to indicate what was
done in each successive box—frame—but a hasty picture using stick figures or something equally easy to produce could also work, especially with
prereaders. Another sixth grade teacher whom I met in my Radford
courses used event frames in her classroom. She said her typically eleven
and twelve-year-old students loved to draw the pictures in each frame and
color them. Time constraints might interfere with this approach unless it
was a homework assignment for a book—a visible book report?

By fourth or fifth grade, stories are more complicated, and there may
be two or even three main characters. With two main characters, a
teacher needs two parallel event frames with the necessary number of
boxes, as shown in figure 3.3. The main characters' names are written in
front of the frames, and the main actions of each are identified. As they
are sequenced, it becomes obvious that the action of one character initiated an action of the other in response, which might bring another reaction from the first character. This can be indicated with arrows leading from one character to the other and connecting the actions
concerned.

If time is short or a story complicated, the teacher can provide the list
of actions for the students to put in the right order in the boxes of the
event frame. On other occasions, the teacher might allow students to
choose which actions are main actions, with or without a hint from the

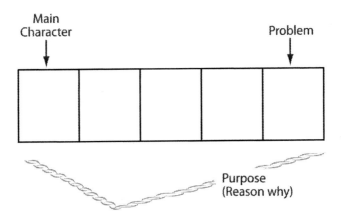

Draw a picture and
write a caption for
each action (box).

Who is the main character?
What did the character do first?
What most important thing did the chracter do last?
What other important actions fit in between?
What reason was there for doing each action?
What problems were the actions working on (to solve)?

Figure 3.2. Fiction event frame with guiding questions

teacher as to how many they should find. "Circumstances alter cases." For younger readers, the teacher may say, "Find five main actions that so-and-so did to make this story happen." The recommendation for an event frame is to keep the number of boxes to ten and under. For elementary school readers, five or six boxes are often sufficient, but a limit of ten is

Story Event Frame (gr. 5+)

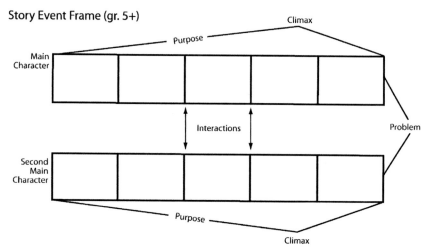

Figure 3.3. Two-character event frame

not too confining. When a character is in a play by Shakespeare, things get more complicated.

There was a nine-year period where my middle school offered a three-year sequential curriculum for identified gifted students. There were four teachers on the team for the four core academic subjects. In sixth grade, English teachers also taught social studies, so in my role as English teacher, I taught sixth grade social studies, integrating with English wherever possible. Then I turned the seventh and eighth grade students over to a social studies teacher while I kept them for English.

When the seventh grade was involved in a theme called "Conflict and Resolution" dealing with the World Wars in U.S. history, in English, we looked at social and personal conflicts and read Shakespeare's *The Taming of the Shrew*. In the eighth grade, at that time, the Virginia curriculum required Geography, Civics, and Economics. During the latter theme, we read Shakespeare's *The Merchant of Venice*. I adapted the fiction event frame for Shakespeare. I included a little scaffolding too, as mentioned back in chapter one.

I provided four parallel fiction event frames for the four main characters of *The Merchant of Venice*: Shylock, Antonio, Bassanio, and Portia. I filled in completely the first and last main actions for each character and provided verbs for each of the intervening actions. Shylock had nine main-action boxes. The first said, " . . . lent money at high interest rates." The second through eighth boxes had verb phrases like "secretly planned . . .

lent Antonio money . . . suggested . . . claimed . . . insisted . . . went to court . . . won, but . . ." and finished with "agreed to sign a paper giving his daughter her inheritance."

The frames for the four main characters helped clarify the plot, both as we read and when we discussed what was happening after we finished reading. Wearing an item of clothing to distinguish their characters, students always read aloud in class with frequent stops to see how we would say the same thing in today's English, but the parallel character event frames cleared up actions and intentions as we worked on the play. Adaptability is the key, and the event frame can really adapt to different situations. Once the concept of a story frame is established, the image of the empty frame pops up in minds of students when they hear *story*, and after a while, it becomes so ingrained, they do not even pull up the mental picture of the pattern.

And do not feel you have to be rigid in your application of the story or event frames. While the three-part event frame is used with young children to emphasize story beginnings, middles, and ends, the very same simple event frame can be used to teach flashback to older students. All you need do is ask, "What would happen if you began telling your story in the middle? Have you ever read a story that started in the middle? How did you find out what had happened up until then? Edgar Allan Poe's story of 'The Tell-Tale Heart,' begins with the *end*. What do writers do when they don't start at the beginning?"

You might take the concept of flashbacks and lead into the problems authors have of writing for the future, as in science fiction or time-travel plots. You can develop lively discussions with challenges such as these, and they do force students to think. And wouldn't there be a writing assignment attached somewhere as well?

From Story to Novel

When students are in middle school, but more likely high school, an assigned novel may be a class endeavor. Even a full-length novel can be represented visually with an icon of an open book, and an event frame that represents the overall plan of the book. In most novels, however, a main event happens in each chapter, and so each chapter has its own event frame, as you will see in figure 3.4. A teacher does not need to introduce the concept of a novel with several examples, discussion, and the working

Novels are fiction books with chapters.
True-life stories are autobiography and biography.
To study one:

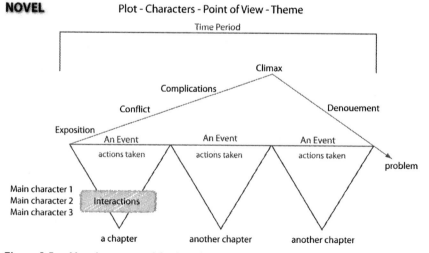

Figure 3.4. Novel pattern for elementary and middle school use

out of a pattern. By this time, the students can check out the pattern, compare the representation with examples of books they have read, and the concept pattern will probably stick. They will remember it quickly, especially if the teacher refers to "the event in chapter four," using the terminology as memory prodders during class discussions.

Older students will learn about themes and point of view, a shown in figure 3.5.

Teachers using literature groups in their classrooms will find they can, and I hesitate to put this so crassly, kill several birds with one stone. The four or five students in each group who are reading the same book will

NOVEL   Plot - Characters - Point of View - Theme

Time Period

Climax

Complications

Conflict   Denouement

Exposition

An Event   An Event   An Event

actions taken   actions taken   actions taken

problem

Main character 1
Main character 2   Interactions
Main character 3

a chapter   another chapter   another chapter

Figure 3.5. Novel pattern with plot, theme, point of view

analyze the events in the book, as well as the characters. Photocopy a single empty frame on an eight-by-eleven sheet of paper, with the bottom part ruled off for a summary-type caption. When the students decide how many important events move the plot of their novel along, you can give them enough empty event frames to summarize the book: one event frame for each important event or chapter. The students distribute the frames among themselves after deciding who will draw and color which frame. You have a bulletin board display when they assemble the finished frames, as a *whole,* for their presentation. That is efficiency.

Creative Writing Planning

The event frame can be used for encouraging creative writing of original stories, too. Students usually ramble in their writing, telling the story they think they want to write as they *talk on paper.* The story is in their heads, waiting to be recorded in the same way they see it. Teachers know the oral tradition needs a bit of help in focusing, and the event frame can be a tool, even if the story only has a beginning, middle, and end, and the kindergarten or first grade student is going to illustrate and color the three parts before telling the story to the class.

They might also make a planning sketch in pencil, picturing the beginning, middle, and end of the story, and then tell it to the teacher, a classroom aide, or volunteer parent who will write it down in the children's own words. This helps youngsters learn the value of planning, thinking things through, and adding enough detail to make a story clear. It helps their imaging skills, and reinforces the idea of stories having three parts to the whole. They have to dictate clear sentences. It is *language experience* all over!

Event Frames for Real Events

When we were in grad school in Nashville, Tennessee, my husband was working full time on a Ph.D., and I was taking master's classes on Saturdays while teaching to get my PHT (putting hubby through, an expression which really dates me on the historical continuum of our changing language). I was one of two sixth grade teachers in a local school and worked with a wonderful woman who was my mother's age. In true Southern tradition, we called her "Miss Ruby." She taught me the value of having students use the information in the textbook to produce something because it required them to consider the facts, relate them, and create a product as the result. I remember two assignments in particular that went with our social studies lessons, which, in Tennessee in the 1960s, focused on the Western Hemisphere outside of the United States' borders.

One assignment was to write the script to show the probable conversation between King Charles I of Spain and Hernando Cortez concerning an expedition to Mexico in the New World. Another was to write the recipe for *jungle bread*.

The latter task was to show how the women in the Amazon rain forest of South America would beat a *bitter cassava* root against rocks to break it into fibrous threads, and then rinse it in the river to remove the poisonous juice. Our textbook did not say it contained *prussic acid,* but an encyclopedia did. When it was dried and ground to flour, it could be baked as a type of bread. Picturing the scene and the actors before imagining the conversations made students take what they knew and reproduce an event of history. I could have used the event frame then.

Event frames require the same analysis of situations to understand the events of history or even current happenings in the news. Students are using information all the time to find out what happened, in what order, and why, and how things turned out. Event frames are miniature time lines, too. The lead-up events, the big deal, and the follow-up situation happen in time sequence, making the causes for the Potato Famine of Ireland or the Sailing of the Mayflower part of the whole picture of that event. Time concepts have always been difficult for middle-grade elementary students, and event frames combined with the use of time lines (which, in themselves, are visual representations of an abstract concept) can work toward helping students understand decades and centuries with respect to their own lifetimes or life lines.

In the case of historical events and their analysis through using event frames, the main character is sometimes a single individual, like a king or an explorer, but can also involve parallel event frames as used with two-character story event frames. The two-character event frame worked beautifully to clarify for sixth graders what the two groups involved in the French Revolution were: the king and the aristocrats versus the peasants. In another case, figure 3.6 shows the flooding and receding cycle of the Nile River and the peasants' way of contending with these happenings.

The Nile River's Calendar

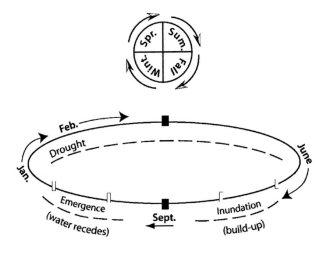

Figure 3.6.   Nile River cycle—event frame

An event frame can summarize the accomplishments of a president's term in office. It can condense the achievements of an explorer, inventor, or social action leader into an understandable size. Just think about the main character in a slightly different way and remember the character can be a group of people who achieved what happened in a recognized historical event. They acted in concert, as one. Think of the Battle of Gettysburg or the Settling of Jamestown. Here is a test question for readers: Which of those event frame topics will need a two-character event frame?

PROCEDURE FRAMES

Frames are great for *schema* representations, and with a little twist in viewpoint, can be used to make assignments that help students by breaking their tasks down into doable sections or steps, something that is difficult for most of them. A student will arrive at home and announce, "Mom, I need to make a picture map of the country of Panama!" He understands the project, what he is to produce, but probably thinks in terms of drawing and coloring, copying from an encyclopedia or atlas, and not much more. And figuring out how much time it will take is not even in the picture for this boy. A procedure frame, shown in figure 3.7, actually provides the conventional scaffolding teachers build into many assignment directions.

The characteristics of the event frame—orderly sequence, left-to-right organization, with further steps building on previous ones—suggest the time required to avoid a last minute crisis at home. It has an advantage over a project assignment where steps are provided, but in list form. Whatever is at the top of a list seems to suggest by mere position that it is the most important. Some students get started, but do not completely finish. Seeing steps in a frame, left to right like a calendar, first to last, where last is *finished*, sends hidden messages. After they have seen enough procedure frames, students know that there is more to this assignment than just to make a picture map. They take them more seriously.

Procedure frames help teachers evaluate the products because the steps delineate what was required, and the project shows whether the requirements were met. Students cannot weasel out of anything this particular time. But it is the help that the stepwise directions provide, which builds up through experience, that gives the student increasing competence for future challenges.

The procedure frame has the inevitable row of connected boxes, but the first box is shorter relative to the boxes for the steps to its right. Above each step to be done to produce the finished assignment are the labels for Step 1 and Step 2, etc. The first, shorter introductory box rates

	GOAL	STEP 1	STEP 2	STEP 3	STEP 4	STEP 5
T A S K	To respond to "choice fiction"	Underline title and center the author's name and number of pages below.	Paragraph 1: Name title and author in intro. sentence. Add 3-5 more sentences to cover theme and plot, or problem and setting.	Check note cards. Organize in order you want to use them. Pile by paragraphs.	Write 2-3 paragraphs describing and analyzing your character. Put page numbers in (...) when you use a book reference.	Conclude with a paragraph about something you learned from reading your choice fiction.

Figure 3.7.   To respond to choice fiction—procedure frame

two labels. Down the left side, vertically, one reads, *Task*. Across the top of the task box, the label reads *Goal*. Read the word, *Goal*, and you know what the end result will be if you follow the steps in the *Task*. From there on, you proceed through the steps to achieve the goal. Reminders, hints, or notes may be added below the procedure frame on the same paper like footnotes. Sometimes, in the case of a major assignment, the traits on which it will be evaluated might be listed for older students. "Be informed so you don't earn a poor grade."

Producing a Procedure Frame When You Need One

Word processors have the facility to create a blank procedure frame that teachers can keep in a file on their computer hard drive. One need only to type in the assignment in a to-form: "to write a report on the Mayan Indians of Yucatan Peninsula," or "to prepare a set of flannel board pictures that tell a folk tale from the nation you are studying." Provide the steps that break the assigned task into orderly parts for the student to follow. Most procedures require only four or five steps. If you use an overhead projector, transparencies of blank four- and five-step procedure frames can be filled in with water-based markers for instant assignments for overnight homework, as you will note in figure 3.8. Or, if you have made a general assignment, you can discuss how to break it down into steps, with the class making suggestions that you will fill in on the blank frame.

And if you are devoted to the photocopier, you can have multiple copies of four-and five-step procedure frames run off as blanks on which you can handwrite or type in the steps to be followed. You could type the steps into the corresponding areas of a blank piece of paper first, and then photocopy the assignment within a frame that you keep on a transparency. That would be one you ruled off using permanent black marker. Put the transparency in place over the typed directions and treat them as a single layer. Photocopy the directions with the lines superimposed on the steps, which will show through the transparency when it is copied. You will find ways that work best for you, but the procedure frame itself works best of all.

Now that we can efficiently describe anything we need to, and analyze any story plot through its characters or any historical event through the groups or persons that influenced or initiated them, we are ready to meet Mr. Egrefs. He is a *cultured* gentleman.

TASK	GOAL	STEP 1	STEP 2	STEP 3	STEP 4	STEP 5

Figure 3.8. Empty procedure frame, five-step (assignments)

4

THE CULTURE BOX THAT
WENT TO COLLEGE

I was teaching overseas in an international-type school that served students from over fifty-three nations, kindergarten through twelfth grade, with an English-speaking curriculum. The students also studied French and Persian (Farsi). This was decades ago, and the school had been started before World War II for Presbyterian missionaries' children in Iran. When I taught there for three years, the school had a large student body with a boarding department for missionaries' children whose families lived in the provincial capitals. Everyone was required to attend daily chapel—Christians, Muslims, Jews, Hindus, Buddhists, and Zoroastrians. It fell to my lot to program the chapel speakers, which meant if someone did not show up, I had to fill in.

One morning I was on the spot and, during the first hymn, pulled out of the air the idea that, according to historians and cultural anthropologists, a people were not considered or identified as civilized unless they had a system of rules or laws, a way of sharing knowledge with the younger generations, and a religion. Now where did I, an elementary education major in undergraduate years, get that erudite standard? It was stated in my sixth graders' social studies textbook. I have always said that, for a general knowledge base, nothing beat the sixth-grade curriculum for a self-contained classroom: math, science, English, reading, spelling, social studies, health, and in this instance, religion, music, Persian (Farsi), and French.

Twenty-five years later, I was introduced to the *culture box*, the visual representation of the instant-chapel talk I had given years before. It *is* a gem. A university professor was even impressed when he saw it for the first time.

Recognizing that no matter how thoroughly you teach anything, there comes a time when you need a mnemonic device. I created one, not unlike ABLGUF, to remember the parts of the culture box: six parts to any whole culture, no matter where you find it, in prehistory, among the ancients, on any continent, or even the North Pole. But hear the explanation first.

Think of our own United States' *culture*, the way our population lives and does things together or individually. We are born, as individual *selves*, and if we are lucky, into loving and stable *families* that care for and nurture us, and even *educate* us to a great extent, before sending us to school for further knowledge and training. In some cultures, the *religion* influences the schools directly; in others, the religious values are inherent in the citizenry and supported through the schools' curricula as social values. The *government* sees to the general welfare, defense, and basic needs, sometimes requiring specific things of the school systems in each state, and putting its influence on the *economy*, the economic system of the nation, which undergirds the whole society.

With the self (the individual citizen at the center) and with five more boxes around the small one in the middle (you can have concentric circles; here you have concentric boxes), you have the essence of any culture established on earth, now, or all the way back to prehistory. The family has always been the social unit, and the family nourishes each individual member, or should.

When I was taking elementary education classes in my undergraduate years, we covered a curriculum for social studies that was called *expanding communities*. Kindergarten and first grade focused on family and *community* helpers, like the milk delivery person, the postal carrier, the fire fighter, and the police. The local community and some in the state were considered. Often, a standard unit on *the American Indian* was included by the time students reached third grade. Fourth grade looked at regions, as *Hot, Dry Lands*, and *Hot, Wet Lands*, in a geographical sense.

How people lived in each type of climate or biome was part of the larger geographical picture. By fifth grade, children were studying their respective states and the history of the United States before moving to the Eastern Hemisphere, geographically and historically, as sixth graders.

Today, children are introduced to other places and other ways of living from preschool television programs, right along with learning letters and colors. Books abound to show *Children around the World* in native costumes, explaining customs, housing, food, schooling, all the elements shared by children growing up, no matter where they are. I remember buying a set of paper dolls of international children as approved by the United Nations.

When using the culture box pictured in figure 4.1, the *self* and *family* boxes are where the basic needs of food, shelter, and clothing are emphasized. Education and Religion also, are touched upon here, and dealt with later as appropriate to the age of the students. Economics can always be approached as work parents do to provide for the family. There are children's books on that topic too. And the John Dewey progressive education perspective of *learning by doing* would insert a classroom store in the play corner, or school store, or a story about a lemonade stand at this point. Older children can see that economics creates differences in providing for children's well-being if the point is not belabored. When they begin to compare brand-name clothing, beware.

Students with enough measuring skills should rule out, in the middle of a piece of notebook paper, a small box, perhaps a half-inch by one-inch rectangle, with half-inch width boxes added all around until there are six boxes, one nested inside the other. Yes, the teacher can provide a blank copy for them, but there is nothing as good for retention as kinesthetic reinforcement of learning. Let them wield the rulers if at all possible.

Working from the outside toward the center, Mr. Egrefs, our cultured gentleman, gets his name from the first letters of the elements of a culture: Economics, Government, Religion, Education, Family, and Self. To put a fine point on it, the culture box, as I was introduced to it, had a red arrow coming from the outside and pointing toward the individual in the center, but also a green arrow from the individual self in the center pointing or leading out to the Economy. That was because we know the culture influences and sometimes limits the self, but the individual self can also influence the culture. Hooray for democracy!

A Culture Box

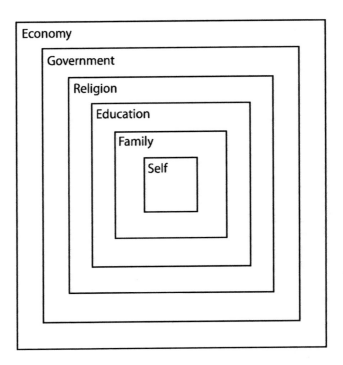

What events caused culture "A" to become "B"?

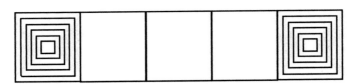

Figure 4.1. Culture box with culture-changing event frame

Now, we have done this a bit backwards, going immediately to the visual representation of culture, the culture box pattern. And, of course, it is easiest to simply explain the pattern, have the students draw it, and begin to use it in class. But the brain is wired to sort through things for matches, both in stored memory and in new things that present themselves. How many elementary, middle, and possibly high school students have a good working definition of the word *culture*? Let us take a serious look at that.

INTRODUCING THE CONCEPT OF CULTURE

I decided to develop a concept of culture as a vocabulary word by using the brain's sorting system and presenting photographs from various cultures.

I visited a travel agent in our town and collected tour brochures and magazines about foreign countries, making sure I had all the populated continents represented: Europe, Africa, the Middle East, the Far East, South and North America, and Australia. I went through them and cut out pictures, separating them according to whether they were photos of single individuals, obvious family groups, school settings, various religious settings, what looked like government buildings, and then things that represented work or businesses. I confess that I put little labels on the back of the pictures to help file them away quickly after the lesson period, marking the labels with continent and cultural aspects to keep track of geographical implications as well.

Sorting the Examples

At this time, our classroom blackboards were magnetic, and I displayed all forty-two photos of all sizes and even some in odd shapes, all over the front board. I used little magnets to spread them out somewhat randomly. I wanted a real mix. Then I invited the class to look them over. I said, "If you were going to organize these pictures, how would you do it?" They quickly suggested putting several pictures together because they had noticed they all had Oriental things in them—people, buildings, clothing, or famous places they knew about. I agreed that the geographic differences were very obvious in most cases and challenged them to find other ways to group the pictures.

That was when someone noticed a photo of a school classroom and another of children on a playground. The student said those pictures could go together because the "kids were at school," and there might be more school pictures. They picked up on the religious photos next, perhaps because there were parallels with the idea of *schools* that helped them form the first grouping.

Things went pretty much according to my plan after that, and while we ended up with a large group with people, and agreed that the picture of the school classroom had people in it, but probably needed to stay with the school group, I pushed them to find a way to separate the people group into two subgroups. A picture of a father talking on the phone while holding his baby over his shoulder and doing something at the sink finally got the parent-and-child-makes-family idea across, and we had the six parts of any world culture represented in the blackboard display. We reviewed the names of the groups we had formed to keep them in mind.

DEFINING THE CONCEPT

All I had to do was ask what kind of a message this sorting of pictures into these six groups suggested to them, and someone obliged me with the winning statement (after all these years, however, I have to paraphrase): *They show that no matter where you go in the world, there are people in families, they work for a living, their kids go to school, they go to church—well, temples or something like church—and they have some kind of government.* Could a teacher ask for more? This approach of sorting pictures from around the world could be done with very young children, too—perhaps emphasizing individual children, and family pictures indicating the housing, some school scenes, and people working. Government and religion could be slipped in later as *other things everybody does.*

Do not forget the books about *Children around the World* that make these comparisons, too. From a book order, I picked up a book called *If You Lived with the Iroquois* (Levine 1998), to mention a more specific culture. Dover Press publishes rather esoteric coloring books. Those are excellent sources.

So there we were, with six groups showing what all people around the world do in their daily lives, and all we had to do was attach a definition. With older students, I would give them examples of ways that we use the word culture in our language. Cities are cultural centers offering cultural activities, educated refined people are often called *cultured,* but when we get sore throats, the doctor takes a *culture* to see what bacteria are making us ill. Biologists *culture,* or grow, *cultures* or clusters of bacteria and other cells in the laboratory. And mixed into the list is a sentence referring to the beliefs, habits, and ways of living of groups of people in various parts of the world. It never takes much debate to select the definition or the sentence using the word, culture, the way we might use it in referring to the groups of pictures we had created.

Adding a Mnemonic Device

I posted a chart with a stick figure whose head is a set of six nested boxes forming the culture box pattern, and the figure is wearing a bowler hat (*veddy* British) and carrying a cane. The chart title says, "Mr. Egrefs is a cultured gentleman." Below the title and the figure is an acrostic poem spelling culture vertically:

Citizens living
Under
Learned
Traditions
Understanding
Readily
Each other

USING THE CULTURE PATTERN

After all those examples, the sorting, the labeling, the defining, the drawing of a culture box pattern in notebooks or consulting a posted model, students were ready to use the culture box in their studies. It was not hard to make good use of it in other subject areas too, like English.

But first, in social studies, we used it to organize notes on various countries we were investigating. And if you recall the two-character story event frame that served to help analyze the two warring groups in the French Revolution, you will not be surprised to note that culture boxes could be used at the beginning and end of a time line or event frame to show how one culture, through a series of society-jarring events, changed into a different culture. Revisit figure 4.1. We also went three-D with it!

A Pyramid of Wooden Nesting Boxes

I was sitting on the couch next to another university faculty wife at a reception when she turned to me and asked, "How do you teach Sumer?" She was a fifth grade teacher at a private school where they used a curriculum that began with prehistory and came up through ancient civilizations to colonial times. That way, when students were ready to study U.S. history, they had a background of why and how it came about. I explained that I had just run into a new way to present world cultures and described the culture box. She was intrigued.

The next time I met her, she told me she was using the culture box and had gone so far as to have the school's custodian build her wooden boxes of various sizes. She piled them up in the classroom with the largest box making an obviously strong foundation (Economy) on which the other boxes rested. She said that the class had drawn pictures of aspects of Sumerian life and put them all over the culture boxes. She did not say what she did with the display when she was testing the students, but she did say no one in the class earned lower than eighty-five percent on the final test. She was sold on the concept of culture boxes.

I admit that I copied her idea and had boxes built for my classroom, too. I covered mine with brown paper, and we glued pictures cut from magazines and brochures to represent cultural aspects. Time was at more of a premium in our schedule, and we did not have enough of it to draw pictures for every culture we studied. Still, the three-dimensional block tower did suggest that governments might influence economy, but they could be strengthened or fall by it also. The individual *self* was at the top of the pile, too, supported by the family; do we not tout the individual and his or her independence?

THE CULTURE BOX GOES TO COLLEGE

Other teachers in my Radford summer classes were using the culture box beyond the history and social studies classrooms. English teachers focusing on assigned readings used the culture box to help students understand thoroughly the settings of Charles Dickens' novels. A unit on comparing world religions focused on a single aspect of culture around the world, something that could be tackled at various points in history, too.

Two former students of mine used the culture box when they were in college and gleefully shared that news with me. One student was taking a psychology course and had to compare six case studies. She used the culture box to analyze the settings in which each individual was living. Another student told me she had to read a novel for a sociology class—I can imagine something like Sinclair Lewis's *The Jungle* for that project—and she used the culture box to organize details about the setting in which the novel's characters were living and working. In both cases, the culture pattern was new to their professors, and the professors were favorably impressed with the way they employed it in their individual papers.

I was interested, myself, in how students used the culture pattern in various ways in my classes. In one instance, small groups studied five or six ancient civilizations and organized notes on a poster-sized culture box for each one. The culture box posters, which I provided, were on different colors to avoid confusion. The groups reported to the class about their assigned culture. It was revealing to hear the way they commented on or questioned the differences between the civilizations, or noted the differences of a particular aspect in several of the cultures. They even picked up on the influence that geography and history have in creating the special ways a people will organize for filling their shared needs. Why were there wattle and daub hovels on one continent, mud brick buildings in one region, or wooden frame shelters, and even stone buildings?

The culture box is one of the strongest visual representations of the concepts that I have used. The cultured gentleman who knows all about individual selves, families, education, religion, government, and economy will serve you well. Think of comparing cultures before and after the nineteenth century inventions of the telegraph and the telephone. Think of comparing the prehistoric setting of the hunters and gatherers and how life changed with the advent of agriculture. This representation of all the elements of any culture at any time will fascinate students and allow them to organize some of the information sent their way on television and video clips on their computers.

5

WHAT DOES A PARAGRAPH LOOK LIKE? LIKE AN OUTLINE?

We have all had learning experiences where something new energized us and gave us hope. Perhaps it was an idea or a discovery that we wanted to share with others because it became so important in our own lives. Sounds like a love affair, doesn't it?

I was so gung-ho on my discovery of brain-based instruction that I jumped right in and tried it with only my initial introduction to the subject at a weekend conference. I had the gist of how the brain worked: the senses take in information, most of it through the eyes. The brain sees examples of something that are obviously similar and decides what they have in common—though conscious thought is not always involved in this, certainly not in young infants' minds. It stores, in long-term memory, the concept it determines based on select representative details. And there it is, for future reference and for comparing to new examples of the *thing* as they are encountered. Simple enough.

DIVING RIGHT IN

One of my first attempts at *concept construction* with a sixth grade class in my middle school was with my average, or grade-level group, although I did have an advanced group in my teaching schedule that year. Because the term, paragraph, was nothing strange to sixth graders—and I was ignoring, for this purpose, how they sometimes divided or did not divide their creative writing or writing assignments into paragraphs—I simply asked one day, "What does a paragraph look like?"

I have never forgotten the sixth grader who was at the older end of the class age-range and who immediately responded (no hand-raising with him), "Like a box with the corner missing," or did he say "taken out"? Bingo! That made sense to everyone, even though typing and computers were fast influencing the field with block paragraphs. Sixth graders did not usually type, in those days.

My first paragraph pattern, therefore, was a somewhat taller than wide rectangle with a chunk taken out of the upper left corner. I passed out photocopied handouts from my Radford class with four small paragraphs on the same sheet for comparison purposes. They are shown in figure 5.1. We checked the shapes—fairly rectangular, and yes, at first glance, the paragraph indentions were there.

Next, it was necessary to ask how they were all alike. One involved Americans being loathe to get out of their cars, and so we had drive-in windows for everything, even had drive-in movies and drive-in fast-food options in the past, and have drive-through pick-up windows and banking windows now. There was a short paragraph comparing cheetahs and leopards—great for science class. There was a longer paragraph on food preservation options, something out of social studies or home economics. And U.S. history was not overlooked. There was a paragraph extolling the importance of the buffalo to Native Americans before the settlers came to the plains. Three paragraphs were indented; one was not.

I do not think I challenged them with a trick question, like "Three of these are indented, but one is not. Is that one *not* an example of a paragraph?" I might have, though, as it was a chance to mention block paragraphing in passing, and how you might not indent a paragraph when you were typing or word-processing. But you did need to put extra space between the paragraphs in the latter cases. Sixth graders usually love to respond to questions or challenges, and I got what I expected: "Maybe you just forgot to indent that buffalo paragraph." "They all have sentences." "They're all about something." Not bad. We refined

Paragraph Examples

A full-grown buffalo weighs almost two thousand pounds. The plains Indians depended on the buffalo for their meat. They made tools, knives, and arrowheads from the bones. They used the horns to make spoons and cups. The hair was twisted into rope. The hides were made into blankets, teepees, clothing, and moccasins. The buffalo meant life to the Plains Indians.

It is easy to confuse cheetahs and leopards at first glance. Both are big cats with spotted brownish-yellow fur. The leopard, which is heavier by thirty pounds, prefers to stalk his prey at night, keeping within the shadows of the African undergrowth. The cheetah, however, likes to search for food in the open spaces of his African home during daylight.

Americans will not walk anywhere if they can help it. They do banking in their car without leaving their seats. They post their letters in mailboxes that protrude into their car windows. They go to "drive-in" movies and to "drive-in" restaurants. To roll down their car window to get something is the way most Americans like to live.

The search for ways of preserving foods is not new. Primitive man learned that he could make foods last by drying them.. The Indians, for example, hung buffalo and deer meat in the sun. The greatest single advance began in 1800 when a Frenchman, Nicholas Appert, discovered that he could preserve certain foods by sealing them in jars and keeping the air from them. The process was the beginning of the vast canning industry which brings us a variety of foods in all seasons. Pasteurizing is another process which delays spoilage. It is of great importance to the dairy industry. Foods like apricots, peaches, and apples are often preserved by drying. The use of chemicals is another method, and some foods are cooked with sugar. But recently the use of frozen food cabinets has grown tremendously. More foods than ever are being processed by freezing.

Figure 5.1. Paragraph examples—four types (Developmental Skills Institute)

those statements and got the usual paragraph definition about a group of sentences telling about the same topic.

You can imagine that the discussion had to continue with my prodding their thinking with slightly leading questions. The sentences had to say something the reader needed to know about the topic. They had to be putting a message across. That point got us to the timeless label of *main idea*. And I might have been guilty of asking them how much information a paragraph should have and how they knew when the paragraph was finished, when it was over.

I do not want to dwell on this too long; we ended up with a list of things that a paragraph had to have in this box-like shape with the corner cut out, as shown in figure 5.2. It needed a subject or topic. It had to have a point you wanted to make about the topic, the main idea. It had to have enough information to get the message or point across, and it had to put the information in logical order so it did not confuse the reader. After that, you had to have a satisfying ending sentence. That was sometimes called the concluding sentence; one year, after being influenced by a new English textbook, we called it a *clincher*, as in "That clinches it!" from conversational English.

I knew that using a pattern like this one might incur the wrath or at least the irritation of some colleagues who were sold on the Writing Workshop approach. That was a Whole Language-type of natural, functional learning for teaching writing. After all, if you display the shape of a paragraph with items illustrated by flags and pennants on a flagpole in the grip of a bodiless hand, it is a natural reaction for the student to think all that is needed is to plug in a sentence for each item on the flagpole. Oh, dear! Teaching a paragraph this way was as bad as teaching the five-paragraph essay. There was no any room for creativity; it made automatons of students, who would just crank out patterned paragraphs of dull text to suit what they thought the teacher wanted.

I knew all that—I had figured it out for myself—but I had weighed the patterns versus express-yourself-on-paper (as interestingly as possible) approaches and had decided it was more important to establish an initial concept of the paragraph. That pattern would provide some structure for those times students found themselves in a tight place—timewise, skill-wise, knowledge-wise—as in an essay test question. We could worry about fluency and style later. I was committed to the paragraph pattern.

A Paragraph

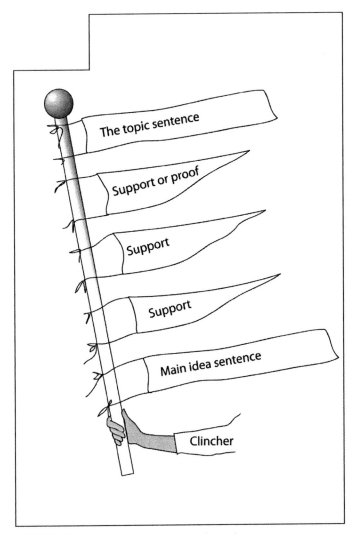

Figure 5.2. Paragraph pattern with flagpole

SO THAT'S A PARAGRAPH—WHAT NOW?

We returned to the buffalo, food preservation, drive-in services, and wild cat comparison again for a closer look. With our definition of paragraph and our pattern, we checked them for specifics. We circled the topics, underlined the message or main idea, checked to see if the last sentence really ended things, and then honed in on the details.

The details in the buffalo paragraph were the parts of the buffalo and how the Indians used them for what they needed. Hm-m-m-m, here's a buffalo and these are the parts of the whole buffalo, but they are also products you can make from the parts. That sounded somewhat familiar. A for Appearance in ABLGUF mentioned the parts of the whole, but Usage was an emphasis on a process to produce a product. We turned to the American's love for the automobile: drive-in banks, drive-through pickups for fast food, drive-in movies (some are still in existence), and drive-by mailboxes. Those details were examples of how Americans used their cars so much they hardly ever got out of them; they were examples of what they did while driving their cars. To connect them to the B in ABLGUF, these examples were their actions or their Behaviors.

The students began to think they could read my mind. So far, the first two paragraphs had details that connected with dimensions of a description, but not the whole description. What would we do with the paragraph on the cheetah and the leopard?

The cheetah and the leopard were two cats, but did the paragraph have two topics? Students thought the definition about a paragraph was sacrosanct, though not in so many words, and they did not think a paragraph would ever have two topics at the same time. I suggested they try another way to word what they had noticed, or find something to say about these two animals besides the fact that they were both big cats.

In looking at the details, the students decided the purpose of the paragraph was to compare the two, and for that you had to describe them. They looked at the details, which talked about color, features like size and weight, and also mentioned both animals lived in Africa and that they liked to hunt, but at different times of the day. Categorizing these details was going to be tricky. They decided the details were basically about the two cats' appearances, but then the paragraph threw in some contrasts in their looks *and* their behaviors.

The last paragraph about food preservation was not of high interest level. It started out too much like a display label in a Frontier Museum when it talked about the Indians drying buffalo meat, but then it came all the way up to modern canning and freezing techniques. It covered the whole range of how to keep food beyond the time it would usually go stale or spoil. The details all suggested processes to make products out of foodstuff, which could be kept a long time.

If a discussion goes on forever, teachers lose student interest, and only a few die-hards will hang on while they can hold the floor. I led them toward the idea that all the paragraphs had details, and they even noticed details could be parts of a complete description, perhaps one or two of the six dimensions available. What seemed to make the difference was the purpose of the paragraph. Why was it written?

The writer of the first paragraph wanted to make the point that the buffalo was valuable to Native American survival, and they used every inch of the animal. There was no waste. They even used the dung for fuel on their hearths! The main purpose was getting the main idea about the buffalo across to the reader. The writer of the paragraph on the American driver used a lot of examples. The two-topic paragraph was really comparing two wild cats in Africa. And that preserving of food paragraph could have been a good introduction to a whole article because you learned different things to do with food to keep it edible longer, but you did not really get much information about the different ways to do it.

It was time to focus the class on the idea that these were different kinds of paragraphs because they were written for different purposes: *a main idea paragraph, an examples paragraph, a comparison paragraph, and a summary paragraph.* I thought we could not get much more out of the paragraph concept; we had pretty much milked it dry.

We did practice with some other paragraphs, circling topics, checking for a main idea, counting the details to see what they were about, and making sure there was a clincher. Somewhere along the line, we found that if more paragraphs were following the one we were looking at, the clincher did not really end the paragraph, it moved you to the next one. Of course a teacher would be ready for a realization such as that and say, "Class, that's what English teachers call a transition! Good for you!" (I might have added that *trans* is Latin for across. I did not do much with my two years of Latin, but my greatest gain was being aware of word roots and how they contributed to word meanings.)

I, personally, did concoct the ultimate paragraph example on a transparency. It had a title, "Life Is a Blast!" It was ruled around the edges to show the rectangle's margins with the corner cut out. It was made up of lots of sentences, each one an example of what people would answer if you asked them about the title. But each sentence started with a *green* capital letter on the first word and ended with a *red* punctuation mark. In fact, all the ending punctuation marks were in red. The first words started each sentence, and the red marks stopped them: green for go, and red for stop. (I was into color-coding.) Use your imagination on the paragraph here. Can you *see* the green capital letters and the red punctuation marks?

LIFE IS A BLAST

"Life is a blast," the poster said. Now what did it mean by that? Everyone will give you a different answer. People tell you about doing "fun things," or they may be describing an exciting experience. Sometimes, it's an adventure they had which they planned. It could be a serendipitous or happy-accident thing that happened. When I listen to people's answers, I get a definite impression. All these things were opportunities taken. Life can be a blast. It is all up to the choices you make.

Finding usable examples of paragraphs is not difficult. Taking into consideration the age, maturity levels, and backgrounds of your students, you might use paragraphs from a chapter in a library book for the appropriate age child, or if old workbooks that used to accompany reading series are still around somewhere, they will have a page or two, even more, where paragraph practice is emphasized. Those will work beautifully because they were planned for the same purpose for which *you* want to use them. For older students, you can watch for short articles or columns in mass media publications. I found an article on beach volleyball being considered as an Olympic sport in a weekly news magazine right after one of the Olympic Games years. Teachers have been teaching paragraphs for a long time. We do have a problem with journalism these days, however.

Newspapers I read now seem to have single-sentence paragraphs, as though the writer hit the return key after punctuating, the way typists used to hit the return key on the electric typewriter to go to the next line. If some bright star in your class questions one-sentence paragraphs in newspapers, slough it off somehow. Of course, high school and college groups might hypothesize the reason for this new style. I am convinced word processing is changing many of our previously held conventions. Ask them what might be the result of this approach if every writer adopted it. But that would really create a tangent for the class focus. Taking that side-trip is up to you. In other areas of the print world, each publisher has house rules for formatting, including limits on lengths of paragraphs.

Do not forget that you can turn workbook pages with paragraphs into transparencies and cut them apart to mark up on the overhead projector as students review what their concept of a paragraph includes. Or if your school has progressed to the latest technology, leaving overhead projectors behind, go to the photocopier and make copies for your students to mark themselves during discussion. You will be teaching them how to work with texts and make marginal notes at the same time!

Notice the blank paragraph pattern shown in figure 5.3, which can be used for planning simple single paragraph reports in primary grades.

FROM NOTE-TAKING TO OUTLINING

One of the things I felt duty-bound to teach to my middle school students was note-taking. We even had a study-skills workshop, with a visiting presenter, held for our faculty before school began one fall. Students were becoming obsessed with using the library computers and the online encyclopedia, and, with a swoop, they hit *print* and had the whole article to take with them. Those with computers at home had it made, they thought. Not seeing too far ahead in the technological future, I thought they needed to learn to take notes by hand for speed and efficiency.

We did a lot of note-taking for social studies chapters via the overhead projector and transparencies because I could face the class and see them as we worked. We talked about main words, leaving out small ones, using abbreviations or truncated spellings, or using symbols, and using dashes at the beginning to show that we were not writing full sentences. We indented the supporting notes under the main points, too. This led right up to outlining. How we arrived at the outline pattern was like the way we determined the paragraph pattern.

Outlines had been my bugaboo in school because it seemed that each teacher, each new year, had a different way of outlining. Letters

A Paragraph

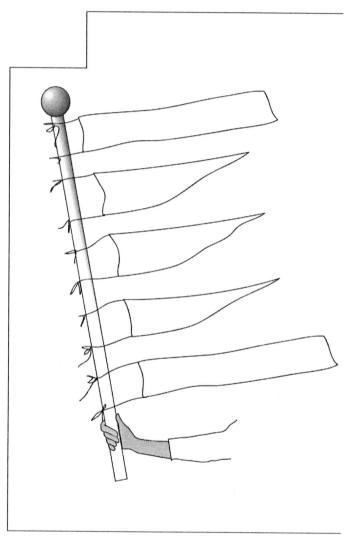

Figure 5.3.   Blank paragraph pattern for planning

were followed by numerals and more letters, or was it numerals, letters, and then numerals again? And now with the *tab* key on the computer, students just hit *return* followed by *tab,* bump the next line over
under the more important outline item above it, and that seems to be
enough.

Purists and traditionalists insist on lining things up just right. Guess where I fell on that continuum. A colleague in the social studies department taught students to take notes and outline on graph paper so they could keep the *columns* straight, or indicate which note-phrase was an important point and which were supporting facts or details underneath. I made a big deal about whether all the numerals lined up and nothing ran into that margin area between the first numeral and the second. I guess that made me an old-lady school teacher, but the object of the outline is the ease of reading it as a guide and organizer for your written assignments.

WHAT DO WE HAVE HERE? AN OUTLINE!

When it came time for me to ask the students what an outline looked like—because I assumed they had been introduced to outlining the previous year, oops!—someone quickly answered that outlines had margins that went in and out. The old reading series workbooks had pages where students filled in omitted parts of outlines provided for the paragraphs on the same page. It was time for me to pull out my trusty chart with the line-framed shape of an outline! It is shown here as figure 5.4.

Limited by chart-space and what I felt I needed to include in this concept model, I had two main topics with their Roman numerals, and the first had two subtopics following their capital letters, the second topic had three. I squeezed in two further supports, the facts or details, with the Arabic numerals under the first letter A, three under the B, and two under the A of the second main topic, II. (See figure 5.4.) There would be time later when we could mention alternating lower-case letters and numerals in parentheses and brackets, just to impress students with the elaborate possibilities for when they were older or in college.

We began using outlining to plan for How-to Speeches where knowledge was usually held in common, and the process was emphasized. How-to Speeches allowed students to get up in front of the class and give their presentation without actually having to look everyone in the eye because they were involved in a demonstration of some sort. A really popular topic at the time was "Making a Peanut Butter Sandwich." Shy students would focus on the action and had an easier time of it, too.

Next, going to the library for short reports involved with social studies topics let the students practice note-taking and putting the notes into an outline form. That is when it happened.

An Outline

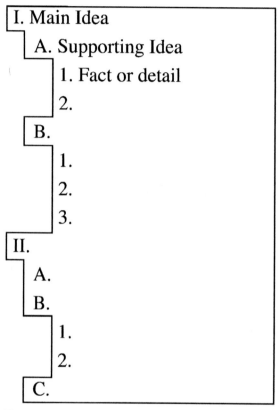

I. Main Idea

  A. Supporting Idea

    1. Fact or detail

    2.

  B.

    1.

    2.

    3.

II.

  A.

  B.

    1.

    2.

  C.

Figure 5.4.   Outline pattern

MRS. LASTER, DID YOU NOTICE . . . ?

I was accumulating chart-tablet-sized sheets of manila tag board for my various basic, curriculum-related concept patterns. I was hanging them above the blackboard around the walls of the classroom—we were beginning to enclose classrooms by now, a return to tradition. In the front of the room, I had the paragraph pattern posted next to an outline pattern. I still remember when a young girl called my attention to something.

She had noticed that the paragraph pattern had a rectangular flag for the topic, a larger one for the main idea, and three smaller flags (triangular-shapes) for the supporting ideas. The sizes suggested the relative importance. "Mrs. Laster, did you notice that the paragraph pattern is like an outline?" The main idea flag had its supporting ideas, and the outline had its main points with supporting facts or details. It was terrific to have a student point out something she had noticed, and to have the rest of the class hear her discovery out loud. It also primed me to prepare a more advanced pattern. That one would visually relate a single paragraph to paragraphs in a basic essay, and show how those paragraphs related to simple outlining. Figures 5.5 and 5.6 show two versions.

Figure 5.5 starts with notes taken as fact phrases, groups them together as topic supports, and then organizes them in a standard outline from which to write the expository paragraphs.

In figure 5.6, there are two outlines suggested. The second one is especially good for speeches and oral presentations since it has four basic parts: A is the introduction; B stands for the theme or topic; C is the bulk of the material as the discussion, and D represents the conclusion.

The concepts I used most in both the English and social studies classes were now concepts to which my students had been exposed and would meet consistently as the year progressed, and as we moved through the topics. But in social studies, there are other visual materials, maps, and timelines.

How to Prepare an Outline for a Report

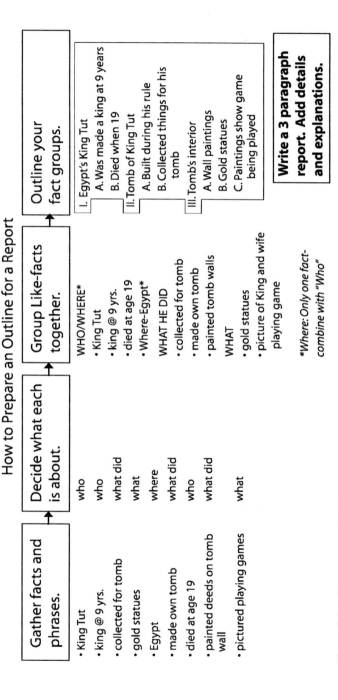

Gather facts and phrases.	Decide what each is about.	Group Like-facts together.	Outline your fact groups.
• King Tut	who	WHO/WHERE*	I. Egypt's King Tut
• king @ 9 yrs.	who	• King Tut	A. Was made a king at 9 years
• collected for tomb	what did	• king @ 9 yrs.	B. Died when 19
• gold statues	what	• died at age 19	II. Tomb of King Tut
• Egypt	where	• Where–Egypt*	A. Built during his rule
• made own tomb	what did	WHAT HE DID	B. Collected things for his tomb
• died at age 19	who	• collected for tomb	III. Tomb's interior
• painted deeds on tomb wall	what did	• made own tomb	A. Wall paintings
• pictured playing games	what	• painted tomb walls	B. Gold statues
		WHAT	C. Paintings show game being played
		• gold statues	
		• picture of King and wife playing game	

*Where: Only one fact-combine with "Who"

Write a 3 paragraph report. Add details and explanations.

Figure 5.5. Notes to outline for a report pattern

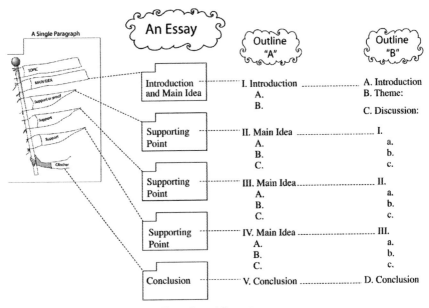

Figure 5.6. Paragraph to outlines A and B pattern

6

THEY ALREADY EXIST!
MAPS AND TIME LINES

When we think about it, there are things with which we have all grown up, and therefore take for granted, that are concept representations in themselves. They already exist. Think of the calendar. With a little motivation and questions like, "When is Christmas coming?" we learned the months of the year. January is supposed to bring snow, February brings Valentine's Day and Presidents' birthdays, March brings spring, April Fool's Day is a favorite with children in school, and, besides, "April flowers bring May flowers," and then it is June, and school is out!

Most homes have calendars on the wall somewhere. As we grow up, the monthly illustrations provide reminders of where we are in the year, even before we can read. Another thing with calendars is the lining-out of the seven-day week in boxes that are numbered, and there are always four tiers of weeks in a month with a few leftover days at the beginning and/or the end depending on which month it is. My generation memorized the rhyme about, "Thirty days hath September . . .," and students are still presented with that rhyme in early grades in many places.

Two images in existence beautifully represent ideas for social studies classes. Child development books used to say that time and spatial concepts were difficult for fourth graders, and as a pre-television generation member, I can testify to that. I read voraciously, and loved history and historic fiction, but in fourth grade, when teachers started talking about explorers in my New Jersey elementary school, it all sounded like adventure stories or folk tales, the fiction I had read. When they threw in the word, *century*, it was definitely foggy information, so unreal.

Children today are raised with television and its newscasts reporting on what is happening all over the world. Children's programming has daily episodes of animated characters who wander to famous places in distant lands or just imagine they do. Geographic distances and the concept of *foreign countries* may not be as strange to our youngsters in the twenty-first century. Still, we do not leave them floundering with only television experiences as background. We have ways to demonstrate both time and space as concepts, and we do it visually.

"Honey, get out the map and see how far we are from that exit we need to take to get to my sister's."

Strapped into their booster seats in the back seat of the family vehicle, children grow up seeing those large sheets of paper with colors and printing, and squiggly lines. They may even ride in cars that have a road atlas as a permanent piece of car equipment. Now we have geographic positional systems (GPS) in our cars (well, some of them), and they display maps and talk to us. Learning to use and read maps is another thing. We, therefore, develop the concept of *a map* in the usual way.

CONSTRUCTING THE CONCEPT OF A MAP

I posted many maps around the room or with magnets on the front blackboard. To sneak in the idea of *scale*, I collected town and county maps, one of our state and one of the whole nation, then a map of the Eastern Hemisphere and the Western Hemisphere, the whole world, and thanks to a subscription to *National Geographic Magazine*, I had a map of one of the poles. I was particularly fond of the world map where North and South America were dead center, and Eurasia had been split and moved to the sides. All I had to do was ask, "What are these things?" The question earned an answer in chorus. "Maps!" But I always asked, "How do you know?" or "Can you prove it?" Preteens rise to the challenge. I imagine all ages of younger school children would, too. High school students might doubt your sanity.

If you had time to spare that day, you could say that the maps were made by *cartographers,* so were they not *carts*?

This is the time to state that throwing in a non-example now and then is a good idea. With the maps on display, I had a floor plan of our middle school and one of a generic classroom so we could start with a small area and move outward to the world. I did not deliberately plan to confuse the issue, but they were there for comparison and to make a distinction between the results of mapping different areas. They helped with teaching *scale,* too. Somewhere along the line, a map of the universe, a sky map of constellations, was encountered, and a map with airline routes depicted. We learned to call those representations *charts.* That would be your connection with *cartographer,* of course.

Many companies that publish textbooks provide a section of those texts devoted to a student atlas of sorts. The teacher may receive complimentary maps that match the smaller versions in the textbooks. During my tenure in the classroom, when the overhead projector was king, there were books of map transparencies that teachers could purchase on their own, and other sets came with the adopted textbooks series, okayed by the state, and selected by the school system. You will be thinking of your own options with up-to-date technologies, I am sure. You could even go to the website for GoogleEarth.com, or Map Quest as twenty-first century resources.

Arriving at a Definition of Map

You can imagine the discussion that ensued as we determined a definition that would be true for all of the maps on display. I think we ended up with the statement that a map was a two-dimensional (*flat*) representation of the earth's surface, or a part of it. That eliminated the school and the classroom layouts. We agreed that *floor plan* was the term for those.

By pointing out that all of the maps looked different even though all were representing the earth's surface or a part thereof, we were forced to look at the details. We had maps of a city, a county, and a state, a nation, a continent or two, and even a map of the Pacific Ocean with groups of islands that functioned as nations. The county map was as big as the paper on which the map of Virginia had been printed.

This is an aside: I was an inveterate collector of comic strips that relate to things I teach in the classroom. I had a comic strip of Bob Thave's "Frank and Ernest," which showed them arguing over a distance on a map. One character asked the other how far it was to such-and-such a place, and was told, ". . . about two inches." I showed my class the comic strip, and we talked about how to tell how long it is going to take you to get from one place to the other using a map. Someone (and, yes, I actually remember his first name: Alexander, not the Great) in a front desk took it upon himself to go up and look at a box in the corner of one map, and he announced that one inch was one hundred miles.

It was time to check a few maps *close up and personally* in each student's textbook. All the maps had a design that looked like a compass and pointed north. There was a box somewhere near a corner that had the map's title—it named the area of the earth's surface being represented—and it gave some colors that represented altitude of the land surface, or symbols that you looked for to identify capital cities, and something it called a scale. Every child had heard his mother or father bemoan added weight when one or the other stood on the scale, but this use of the word was sometimes a new one for children. Take time to list all the ways scale is used in English—from musical scales, to weighing scales, to scales on a fish, or scaling a mountain. But on a map, the scale measures distance the way a weighing scale measures pounds or kilograms.

This idea of scale may call for a separate lesson in another class period when you pass out the rulers and have students measure the desktop to see, at different scales, how far it would be from the front edge to the back edge, or side to side. If a desk is two feet wide, that is twenty-four inches, and if each inch represents a mile, you have twenty-four miles represented in twenty-four inches or two feet.

If that sounds too boring, ask them how far an ant would have to travel to cross their desktops from side to side. Measure their strides, or at least one student's natural step-length, and compare. I know. You will have to imagine the size of the ant step, but ants also come in various sizes. Remember the battle between the red ants and the black ants in Henry David Thoreau's *Walden* (1951, pp. 248–251)? An estimate in fractions of an inch, or even a quarter inch, would be acceptable for ant pacing.

They are not doing scientific research here. They can practice figuring distance on various textbook maps depending on the scale; but for now, just knowing maps have scales will be enough to establish a concept.

Some astute little cherub may also notice that all maps have black lines that cross them from top to bottom and side to side. Perhaps a student will see that the rectangular maps have these grid lines, but the map of the North Pole has lines that curve as though they were going to form a circle.

Think about how you usually do not answer, in detail, all of a young child's questions all of the time, depending on age, timing, and appropriateness of the material questioned. Gridlines on a map and a globe involve lessons on latitude and longitude, and how *lata* means sideways in Latin, for example. For the basic concept of map, it suffices to explain that the lines divide the map into a grid the way streets divide towns so that you can say, "Go two blocks on Main Street and turn right." And indicate that the grid is a special lesson that captains and sailors on ships did not learn for hundreds, thousands, of years. You can introduce them to it later.

Check out this list of the parts of a map, which you see in figure 6.1:

a representative area of the earth's surface
a compass rose
latitude and longitude lines (or just say grid lines)
a legend (key)
a scale

It Is Time to Be Creative

Pass out plain paper and have the students make an imaginary map of an unexplored island that has all the parts of a map but is not actually some place on earth. You *could* say that for centuries people kept finding new, undiscovered islands, but then we put satellites up in space, and they have been photographing earth all the time. We really do not have any unexplored areas left unless they are under the sea, so they will have to imagine an unknown or fictional island. Of course, a couple of newer islands were formed by volcanic explosion, one in the mid-twentieth century, so there is always that possibility.

A Map of Warmia

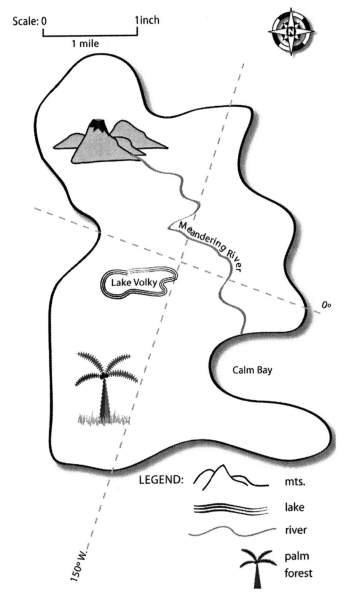

Scale: 0   1 inch

1 mile

Meandering River

Lake Volky

0°

Calm Bay

150° W.

LEGEND: mts.

lake

river

palm
forest

Figure 6.1.   Map pattern

Students usually have a great time making up a name for their island and deciding on its shape and whether it has mountains or desert or features that would be identified in the legend. It is a little tricky when you expect them to mark the latitude and longitude measurements though. If they decide they are on an unexplored desert island, you do not want them using numbers for the grid lines that would put the island near the Alaskan archipelago. You could have them consult a textbook map and pick a spot where the island could be. Then they could use the numbers identifying the grid lines at that point for their imaginary map, their concept of a map. You circulate and help them, of course. The results are each child's personal map-concept pattern.

Each basic concept a child's brain stores begins with a simple, generic image to which all examples of that concept would apply. A toddler learns to say "cat" for a domesticated feline, and then sees that there are tabby cats, Persians, Maltese, and the like. Dogs come in all sizes, colors, and shapes, and have special names for the breeds, in addition to the common pet name the family calls them. And so it is with the map concept. You construct, with the class, the concept of a map from several examples. The examples themselves demonstrate that there are different kinds of maps, and not just the difference in what area of the earth's surface they represent. You have maps that show where humans decided cities and towns should go in their countries, and where those areas begin and end. Those are *political* maps. They are people-determined.

We also have maps that show where the mountains and rivers are, and whether the mountains are worn down or high and still sharp, and possibly which lands are desert or tillable. Those are *physical* maps. *Special interest* maps are just that—maps showing particular information like tree distribution in forestlands for rangers to note, or tourist sites on a state map to encourage vacationing visitors. Population maps represent density through colors identified in the legend.

When teachers start branching out from the initial concept, they are moving into concept dimension. Map concept construction could end with a sorting pattern where all the maps that exist are represented in the large circle at the top like a huge bucket and can be sorted into three, smaller, connected circles for the three types: Physical, Political, and Special Interest. It is most important to establish, however, the initial concept pattern with enough information to make it clear, understandable, and recognizable, no matter what variation the actual content might involve. (Do you hear an echo here?)

Don't Forget to Share

By the way, have the class share their resulting maps, explaining the landform and parts, so each map is checked for accuracy as far as the concept definition is concerned. It is fun to present the finished products. Students are amused by the names of the islands and their shapes, but anxious to check their peers and find them wanting. It is the friendly competition thing. If your schedule is tight, let students share within small groups rather than everyone presenting to the whole class. Shy ones are more comfortable with that situation.

We Cannot Ignore Current Events

International recognition of the looming crisis of global warming and the possible rise of the ocean levels inundating the coastal areas, gave me an inspiration. What popped into my mind when I tried to imagine the coastlines being under water was an idea for demonstrating this visually to students.

What if you had a physical map of a continent like North America, Africa, South America, or Australia—the more regular the coastline the better, that is, few inlets, bays, and deltas—and noted the colors in the map's key or legend representing various levels of altitude? Depending on a four-foot, or the maximum I have heard about in the popular press, a twenty-foot rise of the sea levels, a teacher could cut away that area identified for the lower coastal lines, and students would see where the new coastline would be. Hm-m-m-m. We will have to think about that one. It would be better to have individual maps for each student to cut. Here is a place for teacher collaboration. Science teachers could prepare maps where the future flooding would be shown in a color or cross-hatching, to use an artist's term, making the cutting easier for younger students.

But "seeing is believing," and some people still need to be energized to solve this polar-ice melting problem. I trust you to work on demonstrating that problem as a class activity.

WHERE DO WE GO FROM HERE, AND HOW LONG WILL IT TAKE?

Time, for children, is connected with the clocks in their lives and the schedules they keep. It is very personal. Some children have been so exposed to digital clocks that they cannot tell time when confronted with a clock having twelve numbers and two hands. Do you need proof to believe this?

I had a young lady in the seventh or eighth grade in the gifted program, no less, who never signed out or back in with the actual times when she signed her name as leaving class to go to the restroom. It was a school rule. Someone explained to me that she could not tell time with the kind of analog clock we had in the classroom, and the child herself was mortified. I was sorry that I had made a point to mention the lapse in the sign-out sheet. I saw her privately later and offered to help, but she was probably sufficiently motivated by the embarrassment that somehow she learned on her own. Her parents might have been surprised, too. Yet are we all not surrounded by digital timepieces these days?

When dealing with time in a historic way, someone had the wisdom to represent it in a line. Perhaps they were just listing important events that happened in their lifetimes, back in the early ancient cities, perhaps in part of the Middle East where the Chaldeans lived. They were the ones who came up with base-sixty that we still use for timing and degrees in a circle. And if you think about it, a line is very appropriate. We even use a metaphor for time in referring to our lifetimes as going *along Life's Highway*. We ask, "How long have you lived in town?" "How old are you?" (In other words, "How long have you been alive?")

Pick up any history book, and there is probably a time line in it somewhere. One commercial conglomerate, a company involved with all aspects of media, published a time line series that considered various eras or periods of history and showed what was happening in five different parts of the globe at that time.

There are time line books on history, and time line books on culture—huge, fat paperbacks with six columns that list the years down the edges of the two-page spread. The columns list events that happened in various walks of life: history and politics; literature and theater; religion, philosophy, and learning; visual arts; music; science and technology growth;

and daily life. One example is Bernard Grun's *Timetables of History*, published as a translation from the German. The first edition in 1982 takes history through from 5000 B.C. or B.C.E. to 1978. There are probably updates of this valuable reference.

Time Lines Help a Lot when Numbers Are Too Big

The simplest way to introduce the concept of time lines is to go back to the calendar you thought about when we were discussing event frames in chapter three.

Draw seven connected boxes on the blackboard or white board, or the overhead projector, and ask the class what they could represent. Someone may count seven and say, "A week." You might just start with a blank calendar and cut up a week per strip so you can show one, then another, build up the month, and then attach them for a twenty-eight day month in one long strip. If you have a conventional black board, you can chalk a calendar week quickly. Fill in something that happened on a Monday, a Thursday, etc., to show that memorable things can be recorded to show how close they happened together or how far apart.

If you start with a chalk-drawn calendar-week and erase the top line, ends, and most of each vertical line between the days, you have a line divided into sevenths that still represents a week if your scale is one day per section. That is enough to get across the idea of a line representing time and a bit of the scale-concept, too. You might take an early peek at figure 6.2, a page ahead, now.

If you do not take your own age too seriously, you can ask the class what we mean by a century, and disclose a line you have chalked previously on the blackboard to measure 100 inches. You can ask students how old they are, and draw a parallel line from zero to eight, ten, twelve, whatever (as they say today). You can then reply, "I have you beat." And if it is not *too* long, draw another parallel line to visibly demonstrate the difference in time between your age and theirs.

If your age is something you do not want students to bandy about, ask how old their mothers are, and their grandmothers, or fathers and grandfathers. This is even better because it lets you approach the idea of a *generation* that we sometimes speak of, and how a general rule is four generations to a century. That is a decision you will have to make depending

Time Lines

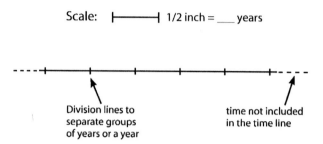

Scale: ├────┤ 1/2 inch = ___ years

Division lines to
separate groups
of years or a year

time not included
in the time line

Time lines represent parts of historic time.

They show a period of time in months or years.

We can talk about time as
  hours in a day,
    days in a week,
      weeks in a month,
        months in a year,
          years in a decade,
  or a century
    a millennium
      a "period," or
        an "era," or
          an "age."

Why not mention seconds and minutes?

Figure 6.2.   Introduction to time lines

on the maturity level of your classes. If you want to pursue the generation concept along with the century unit, you can draw the first stick figure at the beginning of the century and mark it great-grandpa or great-
grandma. At year twenty-five, along comes grandma or grandpa. At
mid-century, the figure represents their parents; at the seventy-five-year
mark, students might be represented, rather small, as starting out.

Ask them how old they would be when the century ended. When they answer twenty-five, ask if that is old enough to become parents, to start a family as the new century begins and do a good job of raising their children. Underscore responsibility.

If you have examples of time lines for teaching that might have been supplied with a teacher's textbook or as a separate poster or transparency, you might post them as examples now, or have students look through textbooks for the various time lines that accompany each chapter of history or social studies books. You can also put that off and give an assignment that works beautifully at the beginning of a school year. It is even a Getting-to-Know-You assignment and will fill a huge bulletin board if you need a display after the first Welcome Back week is over.

Personal Time Lines

Hand out white construction paper of the unlined 12- X 18-inch-size. Show the class a model if you have not given them a procedure frame yet. Hold the paper vertically and tell them time lines can run up and down or sideways. To get all of their papers up around the classroom and have them fit, they will make a vertical time line. Just think of it as a line that *represents* how far they have grown up from the floor since they started to walk.

Ask them about *scale*. How long should each year be? Ask them what would happen if one student used an inch for each year of his life, and another student had so much that she had done to show on the line of her life that she was going to use two inches. Comparison would be difficult. Some students would look as though they had lived twice as long as others. Decide on the standard scale the class will use to keep all personal time lines the same.

Make sure they include at least ten or eleven events minimum. One a year is not that much when you think about it—they are born, walk, talk, go to preschool, are in school through various grades, have annual birthdays, and you are way over the number eleven already. If they add siblings' births, which are important for the changes they cause in the lives of the children already in the family circle, that lifeline will be crowded. And the most interesting events have not even been thought of yet.

Title:
Scale _____ in. = _____ years/centuries

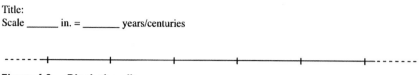

Figure 6.3. Blank time line

Tell them to put a drawing, an illustration or a symbol, by the events and color them in. Neatness is needed for students to be able to read what their classmates have done and tell at what ages they accomplished things. They can ask their parents for help since they probably will not recall when they got their first tooth, for example. If students are grown-up enough to be told to plan in pencil and then ink over for a finished look to the project, try it. We cannot start too soon to encourage taking pride in the quality of our work.

You might already have decided to ask what the parts of a time line are, but you would certainly do that when the individual lifelines are posted and shared. The answers will be a line, numbers for the years, little dividing lines in between, a title, and a scale. They might not think of the scale right away, but someone will point out that it is necessary for someone who reads a time line to know how long a space represents—one, ten, twenty-five, or 100 years, whatever the scale is. If they do not, you must.

And time lines are usually just segments of all the time since the Big Bang scientists talk about. Discuss with the students a way to show the years before and after a *slice of time* you are working with from the historic past. That might possibly elicit the use of dotted lines that suggest fading into the past and the unknown future. Figures 6.3 and 6.4 display a blank time line and one as filled in by a student.

BEFORE WE MOVE ON, LET US RECONNOITER

Here, at the end of chapter six, we should have an idea of how young and growing brains take in and store information in visual concept images. You can make use of normal development and imitate the process to teach concepts in the school curriculum with more efficiency and, therefore, more student success. You have the concept of the six dimensions

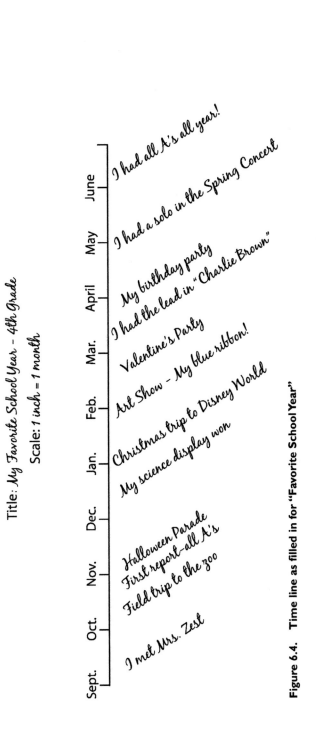

Title: My Favorite School Year – 4th Grade

Scale: 1 inch = 1 month

Sept. | Oct. | Nov. | Dec. | Jan. | Feb. | Mar. | April | May | June

I met Mrs. Zest

Halloween Parade
First report–all A's
Field trip to the zoo

My science display won

Christmas trip to Disney World

Art Show – My blue ribbon!

Valentine's Party

I had the lead in "Charlie Brown"

My birthday party

I had a solo in the Spring Concert

I had all A's all year!

Figure 6.4.   Time line as filled in for "Favorite School Year"

of a complete description (ABLGUF). The event frame is there to analyze and organize the events in stories or in real life, according to the characters or individuals from history who propelled what actually happened. Every event happens in a setting, and every group of people has their own ways of doing things—their own culture. You have a six-part culture box that represents various societies on earth, no matter where they are or when they existed, even if fictional.

Since students use textbooks and fiction texts, and they write about what they know, what they find out, and what they think, you have a paragraph concept pattern (and one for an outline to guide their planning and composing). And this chapter has just discussed the concepts of maps and time lines, without which we could not make sense out of what we teach and encounter in the social studies: history and geography.

What is left under the microscope of learning and memory?

7

YE GODS! IT'S GRAMMAR YOU CAN SEE: THE PARTS OF SPEECH

Teachers have been known to say, "Just because. . ." Among other clichés and pat phrases about teaching, you hear, "Teachers teach as they've been taught." That is usually one of the reasons given for the way school practices have changed so slowly over the years. Before technology speeded up the doubling-time for information to seven years in the 1960s, and five or fewer years since then, the rule of thumb for educational shifts in focus was thirty years—close to a teaching generation, perhaps? I have my own take on that.

My guess is that teachers are generally people who enjoyed school and did well there. If one likes working with children, a person might aim for elementary teaching. Other people are excited about their favorite subject, which became their college major and possibly their first career, and they want to share it with students. They might go into a middle school, but most likely head for a high school or even a college or university campus somewhere.

I was a good student, recognized as brainy by classmates, but I was good at memorizing, and the tests just needed what we called *spit it back* answers when I was in school. I almost decided that I did not learn to think until I taught children. At first, I probably taught the way I was taught at first or the way our very practical college elementary education professor had us trying things out and presenting in class. But having liked school, I am thinking I probably asked students to do things that I remembered enjoying doing myself. Then there were the things I wanted to try, but had not tried before. But do not ask about *papier maché*—the fifth graders loved making a dinosaur in science class the second year I taught, but I never suggested *papier maché* again! We made such a mess!

GRAMMAR IS INTRIGUING

I confess to enjoying grammar. The English language is a favorite interest of mine, having been a reader since the age of three; but I came rather late to understanding the underlying structure, and it was not for the school's lack of trying. I vividly recall the English workbooks we had in my New Jersey school system from third through sixth grades. They all had the same picture on the front, a line drawing of Robin Hood posed in Sherwood Forest in a color that changed with grade-levels. I only vaguely recall green, brown, purple, and a reddish shade, or was there a blue one?

Elementary grammar probably did not make an impression because I had read so much and internalized standard English, even some literary styles, and my parents consistently corrected our errors at home. I could pass tests, as so many did, by thinking about the answer and asking, "Does it sound right?"

My mother believed in taking Latin to get the foundation of languages before taking a modern one, like Spanish. I signed up for Latin I, and for Latin II as well, since colleges preferred two years of a language, and the academic diploma my high school offered then required two years. That was when I learned that grammar counted. I had to teach myself the basics of parts of speech, direct and indirect objects, plurals and possessives, and reflexive pronouns to understand Latin. I had to think through things that seemed so hard that I did not see how anyone ever learned to speak it conversationally, as we speak English and the French speak French. I can still recite the cases though: nominative, genitive, dative, accusative, and ablative. That's all; that's it . . . along with *amo, amas, amat,* and a few vocabulary words. *Puella est pulchra.*

I did get a smattering of sentence diagramming somewhere in high school, but our English courses were divided into six grading periods of this and that: speech, grammar, a yearly Shakespeare play, composition, and literature that included poetry via a publisher's series called *Prose and Poetry*. The first four topics were single grading periods each, but the rest is hazy in my memory now. The fact remains that grammar never impressed me favorably, or otherwise, until college.

Perhaps it was having a stern, old-school, unsmiling, brilliant, and curiously humorous, single-woman English professor who had been an editor of the *Webster's Standard Dictionary* in the thirties before coming to my college to teach. We diagrammed such complicated sentences with multiple clauses. I realized that if I had been taught the rules verbally, for what went with what, and where to put the punctuations, I would not have remembered much. But, to see it laid out on the blackboard or on my notebook page was to see and understand how parts of sentences, no matter how long and drawn out, were related. Things made sense! I was fascinated.

I found myself sitting in meetings with handouts or even in church on Sundays, attendance at which was required way back in time on our Presbyterian Church-related campus, wondering how you would diagram some of the sentences that I was seeing. How would you diagram some of St. Paul's sentences in his letters in the New Testament?

Now I find I am not the only diagramming enthusiast. A former student sent me a copy of June Casagrande's *Grammar Snobs Are Great Big Meanies* (2006). A few weeks later, the chiropractor's assistant spotted me reading it. She immediately told me about *Sister Bernadette's Barking Dog* (Florey, 2006)—a fetching title, that is. Kitty Burns Florey has a poetic way of describing her love of sentence diagramming. "Those ephemeral words didn't just fade away in the air but became chiseled in stone—yes, this is a sentence, this is what it's made of, this is what it looks like, a chunk of English you can see and grab onto . . . And the perfection of it all, the ease with which—once they were laid open, all their secrets exposed—those sentences could be comprehended" (p. 15).

We All Need an Understanding of Grammar

I am not going into battle for teaching traditional grammar. David Mulroy (2003) did that very well in *The War Against Grammar*. I taught grammar my whole career because it turned out to be something I had needed and used throughout my own adult life, not just because I liked diagramming and the way you could put English words together. I also taught it because I expected that many of my students, who would be continuing their educations at a college or university, would need it to study a foreign language in high school—we need lots of translators now—and they need a grammar background in their own language to transfer what they know to the new language. I taught myself a bit to understand Latin, but times change and more background knowledge is needed for just about everything today.

I have had students return to tell me they were glad to have been introduced to a knowledge of grammar. One girl said she would not have learned Spanish in high school and majored in it in college without my teaching of grammar. Another student, who now writes for a nonprofit group, told me never to stop teaching grammar *my* way. The parents of a third student said their journalism-majoring daughter at Ohio University in Athens was required to take a grammar course, but the teacher was only teaching the class what she had already learned from me in middle school.

It's a Global Thing

In his book, *The War Against Grammar*, David Mulroy (2003) points out that most languages spoken by a group of people on the globe today have words that can be grouped into seven or eight classes. As he puts it, "Long experience with a number of different languages has shown that the subdivision of words into eight major groups gives people a good, practical understanding of sentence structure and 'morphology,' or alterations in the forms of words. This taxonomy is the nucleus of traditional grammar. A person is probably competent in the traditional grammar of a given language if he or she can identify the part of speech of each word in a normal sentence" (p. 37). My grandmother would have said that we should all know how to *parse* a sentence.

In these categories of various languages, there are words that name things, concrete and abstract (nouns), words for actions (verbs), for describing things and actions (adjectives and adverbs), words that show relationships (prepositions and conjunctions), and words that avoid repeating the name-words over and over in discourse (pronouns). Most languages have expressions that lack meaning but show a great deal of feeling (interjections): in English we have such expressions as "Wow!" and "What a shame!" In Farsi, there are expressions such as "*A-jab!*" and "*Yah, harahm!*"

Of course there are variations. The third-person singular pronouns in Persian, or Farsi, do not differentiate between genders. One pronoun, which sounds like "ooooh," stands for both he and she. When my sixth graders had a Persian lesson, I never had English lessons or spelling tests right after that. They had been reading script from right to left and would transpose or even scramble letters in a word. And they were apt to use a masculine pronoun to stand for a girl in a classroom discussion. Their classmates were sympathetic, so the error never caused a scene.

Knowing the grammatical structure of our own language helps when we take on another one, even if we only pick it up by ear as we find ourselves in other parts of the world. The brain's organization even underscores the importance of language.

People who have suffered strokes on the left side of their brains find their speech affected. If the blood supply is stopped to an area in behind the left ear, they will still have thoughts, but have trouble saying the words. Damage in front of the ear makes organizing words in a grammatical way to form sentences difficult or impossible (Sprenger 1999; Springer and Deutsch 1981). The brain is wired for language, and that means for both vocabulary and grammar.

Who Is Teaching Grammar Now?

Many teachers groan when you mention grammar and say they hated it in school. They either do not teach it at all or teach it in the Writing Workshop approach at the teachable moment. When they see a number of students are having the same problem in their creative writing, they stop the whole class and teach a three-to-five minute mini-lesson. This is called the functional approach. When asked about the six-week grading-period concentration I had received as a high school student, my doctoral program advisor from the English Department at George Mason University told me it was probably better to teach grammar throughout the school year. That is what I was doing. It was nice to have my opinion validated.

It did not help to have a national convention on creative writing and composition, in 1965, announce research that found that teaching traditional grammar made no positive improvement in student writing. That was the exit door for many teachers and language supervisors. They left the grammar-room and went into the writing-room. The linguists made some impression in the latter part of the sixties with Roberts' series of English Language texts presented from a linguistic view, but that did not last. It is difficult to move people who have been trained to use certain terms and ask them to change those terms, such as calling adverbs "qualifiers" instead of "adverbs."

There were other hangers-on to the grammar banner, other teachers (usually from my generation) and college professors. There was even a brief attempt to organize the grammar-teachers nationally right in my town; I lost track of that one after a couple of years when the organizer and motivator left the university English department for another campus. I did not keep up with the group. According to David Mulroy's book, they now exist as a part of the National Council of Teachers of English as ATEG: the Assembly for the Teaching of English Grammar, with several hundred members. They are on the web.

TEACH VISIBLE GRAMMAR

To teach or not to teach grammar might be your choice or dictated by the state requirements. I chose to teach grammar the usual way until I found brain-based instruction. Remember, the brain sees closed shapes more quickly and clearly than text on a page. Readers spot a picture, a graph, even the numerals forming a year's four-digit date before the eyes settle on the print. From my time with Dr. Fulton, I learned shapes, a sort of logo, for each part of speech. Study the shapes in figure 7.1.

By now, you know I will mention transparencies, and you should be automatically shifting to think of your own available options to project this next visual-teaching chart.

Nouns, Pronouns, and Adjectives are all based on the oval. I am going to describe how I introduced these shapes to my students, but in advance, I made a "Parts of Speech" chart as a classroom reminder. For the noun, I had three oval picture frames hanging on nails. One held a picture of the

You can't say a word without 'em!

PARTS OF SPEECH
(eight!)

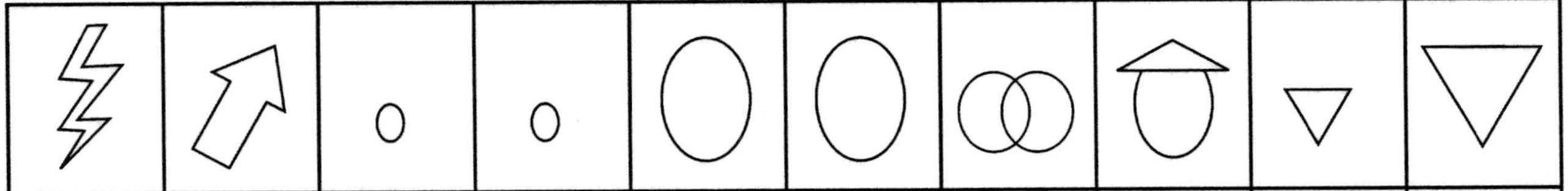

	Wow!	Into	a	slimy	puddle,	Barry	and	he	quickly	sank.
	Interjection	Preposition	Article Adjective	Adjective	Common Noun	Proper Noun	Conjunction	Pronoun	Adverb	Verb
	shows feelings	relates	signals sounds	tells: which? how many?	any person, place, thing	a specific person, place, or thing	joins or connects	takes a noun's place	tells: how? when? where? and sometimes why?	shows: action or state of being
				what kind of?	who? or what?	who? or what?				

Figure 7.1. Parts of speech chart

stereotypical grandma, another of a skyline of a city with a sign pointing
to it, and the third held a lightbulb. That picture frame did double-duty.
The lightbulb is definitely a thing, but it is our society's symbol for an idea,
for an "Aha! moment" when we see the light and understand something.
Cartoonists have used it for years and may still. Once the oval is established for Nouns, you can put a hat on it for Pronouns.

When I started to present the shapes, I used a transparency with various sketches. I would cover up most of the transparency and leave the
portion I was working with exposed on the overhead projector. I showed
an oval in outline only and asked students to use it to make something,
to add details to make a recognizable picture. Most made faces, but that
worked into my plan since nouns name persons. After sharing what the
students had drawn, I disclosed the sketches for a person, a map of a
town with an oval beltway road, and the lightbulb. Might not Edison
have framed a photo or picture of his invention that had such an impact
on daily life and have hung it on his wall? In figure 7.2, a picture of a
restaurant sign represents a place.

We have a line of poetry, "A rose by any other name . . . " (from Shakespeare's *Romeo and Juliet*), and also an idea from minimalist staging in
theater that a change of hats can suggest a whole other character. "He's
wearing his chef's hat now," a wife says to her guests about her husband
holding sway in the kitchen. The costume box in a preschool and kindergarten classroom will have various hats for children to wear during dra-
matic play. In the chart, the oval with a triangular hat that looks like a
woven sun hat worn in rice paddies by Asian harvesters represents another name for a noun, a Pronoun.

One of my middle school students picked up on the prefix and emphasized it with a modern sports twist: "It's a pro-noun, a professional
noun!" But all ages of students can readily recognize the needed efficiency of pronouns if you read a paragraph and change all the pronouns
back to repeating the name of what it represents, the antecedent. Or
just tell them a little story about yourself, someone in the class, or an
imagined relative, such as follows:

> . . . Aunt Sally came to visit my family. Aunt Sally brought the children
> presents, and Aunt Sally gave them to the children after supper. The chil-
> dren showed Aunt Sally where Aunt Sally would sleep during Aunt Sally's
> visit, and so forth.

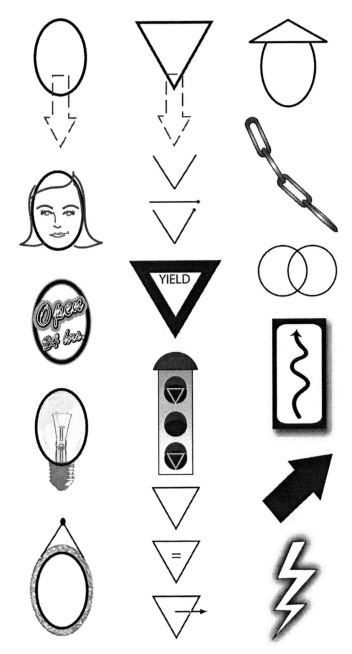

Figure 7.2. Sketches for introducing symbols

You might even have students take a paragraph and put all the pronouns back into the actual nouns they were replacing, and then have some paragraphs read aloud to demonstrate the impact. Gradually, it will become apparent that we have pronouns for people and things, and they can be possessive without apostrophes, and they might change forms depending on where they come in a sentence. It may also become apparent that clear antecedents are needed.

An old 1950s talent show with host, Arthur Godfrey, used to open with a question for each guest, "Whom did you bring us this evening?" Mr. Godfrey stressed the *whom* to correct the oft-made error, "Who did you bring?" *Who* is a subject pronoun, but in this question word order, *you* is the subject of the sentence. The idea of the difference between subject and object pronouns may require more language maturity than classes of primary and elementary students have. You could tell them that Who does the action, and Whom has the action done to it. (And now how many of us are thinking of Abbott and Costello's "Who's on First" clown-act?) We could say that Who does the actions, and the actions are done to Whom, but that suggests a "who-beat-up-whom?" line of thinking. They really only need to know the term *pronoun* at this point. (See Note 4.)

The final use of the oval form is for the Adjective. If a tall oval is the noun, then a short oval by its side is an adjective, since adjectives and nouns go together, a phrase that appeals to preteens and teens for its social connotation. I lump articles in with adjectives as they also modify nouns. A girl can say, "That's the one for me!" or she can emphasize her emotions and say, "That is *the-e-e-e* guy for me!" All other male friends are just boys or boys that she knows. Articles can definitely modify your understanding of the relative importance of the noun that follows when used with such inflection.

I might add that I draw all the symbols for nouns, pronouns, and adjectives in the color blue. Yes, I color-code grammar without too much reference to the colors at first, just as an added layer of information the senses can pick up and send to the brain. Blue is a *cool* (not warm) color, one of the primary colors, and besides, I need red and green for another part of speech.

Toddlers learning to talk learn nouns first as they learn names for things in their environment, but it does not take long before they are adding actions. "Baby go bye-bye," a toddler might say, while standing and pushing at the door because he wants to go outside. Actions are Verbs in grammatical terms. For the symbol, I took Dr. Fulton's triangle and turned it upside down because that way it was a V for verb, and you could simply close it off across the top. It was also the shape of a yield sign at the entrance ramp of an interstate highway. What does a driver do at a yield sign? She might slow down and look, stop and wait, slow down and enter the lane, move over when space in traffic allows, speed up to join the traffic flow—all actions, all verbs.

I drew a traffic signal with a red triangle in the red-light area and a green triangle in the green-light area. What do you do at a red light? You stop and sit there and do nothing. You wait there. You just *be*. You might be tired, frustrated, relaxed, impatient, but you are being in those states or conditions. The light turns green, and you step on the gas and release the clutch if you are driving with a gear shift, you steer, you think about where you are going, and you watch for cars still in the crossing area. You are moving and acting out motions and behaviors. Presto! You have built on the concept of a traffic light to explain action versus being, or state of being verbs, and you have introduced a color code you can quietly use in future lessons: red for being verbs and green for action verbs. "Go, girl, go!" Yes, "Go, guy, go!"

And do remember, we are using a smaller inverted triangle for adverbs describing or modifying the verbs they accompany. Generally you find yourself using green more than red for verbs and adverbs. But it does not do to get too involved in how consistent you are. Green means go, and go is a verb.

Prepositions somewhat define themselves. They never stand alone. They are positioned "pre" or before the noun that finishes the phrase and makes sense out of the preposition. I had taught a good many years before the librarian in our middle school pointed that out to me. These days one does hear incomplete prepositional phrases. "He's coming with . . . " a mother might say of her toddler son, meaning, "He's coming with me." But for English language study and appreciation, we will not recognize contemporary colloquial phases that we hope will pass soon. "I'm going through . . . " immediately raises the question, "Through what?" Are you going through surgery, a rough time right now, a traffic tunnel, a divorce, or through town on your way to visit your parents?

Prepositions are in a pre-position to a noun object that answers the question "What?" The arrow symbol pointing behind, toward the identified word, says, "I'm a preposition, because I'm in front of, or coming before the word that completes my meaning, and forms a phrase, usually two or three words. Notice what is behind me."

With prepositions, and the conjunctions that follow, you can get very involved if you want to color code. You might want to show that a conjunction is joining two nouns, and use blue for that conjunction symbol; you might be using a conjunction to join two verbs, and then you would pick up the green pen. And prepositions are equally tricky for the person who wants to do it precisely right. You would have to use blue for prepositional phrases acting as adjectives, and green or red for adverbial prepositional phrases. Some things can be too complicated. Color code if it suits you; color code to make a point; color code from the beginning, especially with verbs, until students are clear about the difference. Then relax.

A pretty, young blonde sixth grader had trouble with prepositions, often lumping them with the verb or verb phrase. Surely English does throw us some seeming contradictions. At Thanksgiving time, we sing, "Over the river and through the woods to Grandmother's house we go!" Over is a preposition children have learned from the children's educational television show, *Sesame Street*. You can go over and under and through, and around and between things. But if someone asks you to look over a letter, you do not hold it up to your eyes and peer over the top. What looks to be a preposition is actually part of a two-word verb: look over. And so we developed a rhythmic chant, which today might be called a rap.

We chanted, "A prep-o-si-tion starts a prep-o-si-tion-al phrase." Accent the *prep-*, *starts*, and the *si* in prepositional, and *phrase*. Imagine scanning that as a line of poetry if the rhythm escapes you at first. Figure 7.3 notes it in musical terms.

A preposition starts

Figure 7.3.   Preposition—chant or rap

Conjunctions are joining words, glue words. Dick and Jane and Baby Sally did things together in my first grade readers. We talk about every "Tom, Dick, or Harry." We say, "I choose this one, but not that one." A chain link joins itself to the next link, and as anyone who ever made a paper chain for holiday decorations knows, you can add as many links as you want to. As long as you glue or staple them securely, they will hold a link on either side of them quite sturdily. The symbol for conjunctions becomes two links in a chain. Three links might have been closer to representing actuality, but two links take less time to draw or sketch. You have to be practical.

Does that bring us to the last of the parts of speech symbols, the one for the Interjections? Dr. Fulton did not include a symbol for Interjections, as I recall, but I just had to finish the set. I decided on a lightning bolt. During a storm, you see lightning flash, and once you learn in science class what it represents, you start counting seconds to see how many miles away the storm is. If the lightning flash and the thunder come almost right together, you say, "Whew! That was close!" Or you might yell, "Ouch!" or "Wow!" in fear or shock. But you do feel something in the presence of lightning, and that became the symbol for strong-feeling words for my purposes.

By now, we had the chart on the wall or the chart stand, a chart the students drew for their notebooks, and even a set of laminated and color-coded shapes large enough to put on the bulletin board. These could be arranged in rows as puzzles for the sentences they might represent, and students could be challenged to write sentences that fit the symbols in that order. We were ready for grammar lessons (See Note 5.)

Using the Symbols

It should be easy for teachers with some years of experience to remember the English series that had exercises where students parsed sentences, word by word, and put N over nouns and V over verbs, Pro over pronouns, and Adj or Adv over modifiers. (It might have been one published by the Laidlaw Press.) Prep and Conj served for prepositions and conjunctions. I was sharing Dr. Fulton's symbol system with English teachers at my school on one occasion, and a very experienced older teacher who worked with special education students asked if using symbols did not simply require students to learn a second language, as it were? The teacher made a valid point.

In my years of experience with this approach, that has not been an issue. To the contrary, the intangible concept of grammar is transformed into visible symbols, easily recognized and understood. The brain spots closed shapes faster than just mere printed letters or scripted handwriting. The symbols are learned quickly, especially if the teacher is consistent in using them and has charts and bulletin boards to which students can refer, and they are a big help in analyzing sentences where a compound subject or a compound predicate will stand out starkly with two ovals or two inverted triangles. Take a leap of faith and try them. Some students are such visual learners that you may open for them what has previously been a door into a room of confusion.

And to put a coda on that aria, researchers have found that learning a second language before puberty is easier and usually learned with the true accent of the native speaker. Symbols are a lot easier to learn than a whole language, but while I am identifying the benefits of learning a second language, I must not overlook mentioning that research shows children who are bilingual, or learn a second language early in their lives, do better in school than single-language students. Researchers hypothesize that the children become more flexible thinkers (see Domenico Maceri's article online at *People's Weekly World* website for January 8, 2004). Do not avoid the symbol system because it is another language to learn. Look how fast we learned the international logo for restrooms. Many tourists were saved that way, and they were adults.

Poetry as a Mnemonic Device

My husband's mother taught school, too, and had a wonderful little spiral-bound book called *A Living Grammar* (Watson and Nolte, 1955), which had been first published in 1938. In it was a poem called, "The Parts of Speech" (pp. 2–3). I confess that I actually had my sixth graders learn the poem and write it from memory in class as a quick little test. I thought it would help them if they suddenly found themselves asked in a future English class to define a preposition or an interjection and they froze for a moment.

. . . NOUNS are just the names of things,
   As rice, and birds, and snow, and rings.

The ARTICLES are the, a, an;
They point out nouns: the boy, a man.
PRONOUNS take the place of nouns,
As she for woman, they for clowns.
ADJECTIVES describe the nouns,
As quacking ducks, and pretty gowns.
The VERB some action names, like stir;
Or state, like is, or was, or were.
Something is done: the ADVERBS then
Tell where and why and how and when.
A PREPOSITION precedes a noun:
By, at, from, to, or in the town.
And, or, and but join words and clauses,
CONJUNCTIONS—used instead of pauses.
Strong-feeling words are Ouch! and Oh!
They're INTERJECTIONS: Ah! Bah! Lo!

Somewhere along the line, I omitted the word *to* in the original preposition couplet above because it put an extra beat in the rhythm of the line.

Don't Forget the Silly Stuff

From a colleague who had had a demanding English teacher herself, I learned a list of helping or auxiliary verbs. I made a chart of them to post when we were studying verbs and verb phrases: do, did, does, has, have, had, would, could, should, might, and must. I hope I did not leave one out. But my colleague also had had to memorize a list of being verbs, and while I am not a proponent of memorizing everything, there are certain bits of information, even some historic dates, that it helps to have memorized for a frame of reference when you need them. With the emphasis on sports in this country, it was natural to put a little rhythm into the learning of the list to help the memorizing, and we ended up with a cheer!

"Let's cheer the being verbs!" We bent our elbows and curled our hands over into semi-fists; we moved our arms alternately, and we sing-songed: "Be, Been, Being! . . . Is, Am, Are, Was, Were! Rah!" At the beginning of using this cheer, I would add, as an aside, "But Rah! is not a being verb," as a reminder. Soon the students were adding that little reference at the end as they spoke the cheer in chorus, and they were adding it in the same aside-style with grins on their faces. They knew I would be worried that they had memorized an error. And I was, the first time it happened.

When we were focusing on pronouns, we had another cheer. If you ever had a yen to be a cheerleader but were afraid to try-out, you can become a teeny-bopper for a few seconds with the pronoun cheer. With left elbow bent, and hands in the loose-fist position, thrust your left fist out and firmly say, "I." Next your right fist comes forward with a hearty, "You!" Back to the left with enthusiastically urging, "He, She" and finish on the right with "It." Back to the left to holler, "We." Again on the right, insist, "You," and then, "They!" with your left fist, so you can end with a hearty "Hey!" on the right. But as you cheer, "Hey!" turn both palms outward and move them in a circle. It is a flourishing ending instead of a huge, four-limbed spread-jump.

One caution to remember, though. Be sure there is a subtle break— a glottal stop?—between the *she* and the *it* in the third person singular. If you glide through the vowels, you will sound like a Southern farmer reacting in frustration to a barnyard instance, and the students will react with gasps and then guffaws. Classroom decorum will be lost and lesson time, too. The shift from left side to right might disguise this potential *faux pas* for all practical purposes, but you should be careful anyway.

One academic year, a student asked if the class would cheer the object pronouns. I said, "Probably not, but what would they sound like?" We went through the pronouns that were never subjects doing the action: me, you, him-her-it; us, you, them, and ended with "Ahem!" to round out the rhyming end, as in "they and Hey!" That instance was a bit exciting because it was a situation where a student took what he knew (a silly cheer to bring laughter into the classroom along with a rote learning piece) and applied it to something new but related—another chance to interrupt a lesson with laughter? All teachers have signals to reinstate class order, and it is better to laugh with them and enjoy learning than to keep a straight face at all times.

Trigger Songs

I recall a young lady who was flustered by the term, *predicate verb*. From somewhere in my memory, I pulled up a folk song or children's song tune that had a similar rhythm as in predicate verb (think: dah-da-da), and we learned to sing,

> . . . The predicate verb is the action word,
> The predicate verb is the action word,
> The predicate verb is the action word.
> If you can't remember that,
> You're a bird!

It had a nice bounce to it. They picked it up quickly, and we rarely had to sing it. It is shown in figure 7.4 if you are musically curious.

Another song that served to emphasize prepositional phrases was a camp song I learned from my mother, *The Yankee Soldier*. Not only can you point out prepositional phrases in these lyrics, but there are two non-exemplars as well: *to know* and *to go*, infinitives of verbs. The text for this one went:

> Around the corner,
> And under a tree,
> A Yankee soldier once said to me:
> 'Who do you think will marry you?
> I would like to know.
> For every time I look at your face
> It makes me want to go . . .'
> Around the corner . . .

And you repeat the song again, possibly *ad infinitum* or *ad nauseum*, if that comes first. The melody line is shown in figure 7.5.

Other versions of this song exist, but stick with this one for the prepositional phrases. (See note 6.)

You might make up your own lyrics for a familiar tune like, *Happy Birthday*, which is known and sung worldwide. A group of upper-grade students might like trying their hands at creating the lyrics using the prepositions of their own choosing. I got this idea from a librarian friend of mine. It is a winner!

The value of the two aforementioned songs is found in the simple reminder they provide when you lah-lah-lah the opening phrases, without singing the words. It becomes a hint to some student who is pondering

The Predicate Verb

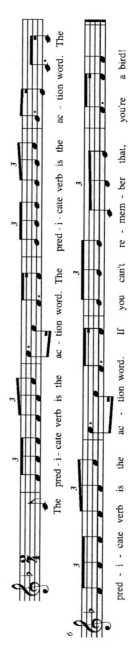

Figure 7.4. Predicate verb song—melody line

Around the Corner

As sung by Mildred S. Travis

Figure 7.5. *Around the Corner—melody line*

an answer but not getting it. The auditory memory of the melody brings the language of the lyrics right along with it.

Not so silly was an assignment given the eighth grade students in my son's English class. The textbook had a list of common prepositions, and the assignment was to include as many of the prepositions as possible in phrases and illustrate them in a scene on a poster board. Scene equals visual. The phrases represented were listed in a key across the bottom of the colored picture with numerals to identify them in place on the picture itself. Choosing a scene that would allow using as many prepositions as possible was a challenge. From there on, it was often fun because things could be portrayed, for example, as happening on London Bridge, over the bridge, under the bridge, and off the bridge with laughable results. Artistic talent was not a prerequisite, but neatness helped.

Practice with Games

Remember that party game where they passed around a piece of paper, and each person in turn wrote a word on the paper and folded it over so the next person could not see what had been written? Someone would call out a part of speech for each word, and after seven or eight words had been written, the last person to write a word read the sentence to the group. It was largely a nonsense sentence, but it was grammatical in most cases, and provided a lot of silly laughter. I am guessing that it came from the popularity of a grammar game in pad-form, called *Mad-Libs*, offered by school book clubs. Paragraphs had blanks to fill in, with the part of speech assigned in small print under each line.

Sometimes older students and adults played a variation where the participants took turns writing a line of poetry, folding the paper over, but writing the last word of the line of poetry, which was now out of sight, on the next line to help with rhyming. The finished sets of six to eight lines were read aloud. Some would be surprisingly poetic. Save that game for a poetry unit. Stick with the simple approach for teaching grammar basics.

Team Competition and Board Work

Once students have rudimentary understanding of the parts of speech, teachers can use the folded paper game above, or an adaptation of it, which also works in classroom competition. Use each row of student desks as a team and have the students write the words on the blackboard one at a time. If you group students around tables, you can pass a paper around the group. You can also have the first student write a word on the board, the second add a word, and the third, and so on, until the result is a complete sentence.

When the class learns that points are received for coming in with the first sentence, but the teams earn bonus points for the number of words it took to form a complete sentence, you can see the minds working, calculating—ten points for a first win, but if each word is worth two points, is it better to try for a short sentence to come in first, or a longer one to amass more points? The deal with this game is that they cannot plan a sentence ahead. Everyone in the team has to work with the word that the first student writes on the board, and everyone must put up his or her own choice of word without hinting to the rest of the team the sort of resulting sentence the student had in mind.

Now you are practicing parts of speech but moving into sentences. That is another chapter—possibly the last, possibly not.

PUTTING IT ALL TOGETHER:
THOSE CLAUSES AND PAUSES

The top line of the Parts of Speech chart says: "You can't say a thing without 'em." And that is the truth about any language, your own or one foreign to you, one that you are trying to learn. You can memorize labels for things and words for various verbs, but putting them together in grammatical sentences that represent idiomatic English, French, German, Spanish, Chinese, Arabic, Hindi, Swahili, et al., is quite another matter. Now, in chapter eight, we put words together in sentences to depict the sense of language.

SENTENCES: KINDS AND STRUCTURES

Actually, a formal introduction to sentences, if presented in a brain-friendly way, will begin with a number of sentence examples a teacher shows to the students. It helps if they are not presented as parts of a typed set or separated sentences from a familiar story. The first impression, or even an element of surprise, is important. I used to make transparencies from magazine advertisements because the sentences were often in slogan form, strange letter styles or fonts, and occasionally were not punctuated. A collage of such clippings on a poster board would work the same way if the class could come up close enough to the poster to read them. And teachers can ask students, "What have we here?"

For discussion, these are examples I used. One advertisement used a pair of sentences: "He likes oysters." "She like pearls."

Another one used: "Diamonds are a girl's best friend." "You have enough friends."

Usually the clips were single clauses:

"So much is riding on your tires."
"A woman's place is in the home" (quoted, no period)
"What does a great detective look like?"
"Buy one; get one free."
"What's it like to constantly feel the pressure of life in the fast lane?"
"So look what I created with ricotta cheese!"

Unusual sentences also distracted students from guessing what the teacher intended. They did not start out automatically feeling bored: "Oh, more grammar." The initial impression of the examples was that it was not something from an English lesson. Often they recognized the original advertisement, especially if it had a counterpart on television.

But a teacher can press a class, saying, "Yes, it's a phrase from the ad for such-and-such, but what else is it?" Eventually, you will get *sentence* as an answer because they do know they are in English class, and you can hope that someone will notice one that qualifies as a sentence, but was not punctuated in the advertisement—maybe for artistic purposes? Of course, you will have to decide what all these examples of sentences have as traits or characteristics, *parts* of the whole, that make them sentences.

It helps to have a mix of standard sentences for the first group of examples so you can construct the basic concept of a sentence as a complete thought; the speaker has something to say about a topic (subject, and predicate or verb). It may be time to ask, "What does a sentence look like?" Or it may be that you need to ask, "If a sentence is a string of words about a subject that makes complete sense, what shape could we use to draw something to represent it?" I have discovered a rectangle works best.

A long, low rectangle divided into two parts by a vertical line in the middle does a nice job of representing the simple sentence. The rectangle could be a half to five-eighths inches tall and three inches wide, but drawn much larger on the chalkboard. Ask the students why there are two sections to the rectangle that represents a simple sentence. You should get the answer, "One for the subject, and one for the verb (or the predicate)." This is when you draw an oval in the left-hand side of the rectangle as the noun subject, and the inverted triangle for the predicate verb in the right-hand side. If you want to, go for overkill and print an S inside the oval and a V inside the inverted triangle. That is your basic sentence pattern.

This sorting pattern for all simple sentence possibilities is a bit premature here, but since we are emphasizing visual image storing for learning and retention, I am going to ask you to study this pattern, as shown in figure 8.1, focusing on the four options under the huge circle. Think of the circle as a bottomless well of possible sentences. No matter how many you bring up in the bucket, they will be of four basic types. Keep the divided rectangle firmly in mind as the discussion proceeds, and the variations will be easy to remember.

A long, long time ago, when you could count on most of your students going to church and Sunday School with their families, I would ask them if anyone knew the shortest sentence in the Bible? I would explain that when I was a child, I had a *Bible Lotto* game that my mother's friend gave me; it had lots of questions on small cards that you used to cover the answers on your large game card. It was a variation of *Bingo*, a gambling game made socially acceptable, perhaps. The last fifteen years or so before I retired, I would just mention the *Lotto* game and tell them one of the questions was: "What is the shortest sentence in the Bible?" If anyone knew, I certainly called on them to answer, but usually I just said, "It's 'Jesus wept.'"

If using religious topics in a classroom makes you uncomfortable, just point out that the sentence pattern makes it look as though we only speak in two-word sentences, and ask if anyone knows one. It is funny to stage a conversation where the people are limited to two-word sentences. After a few two-word sentences, you can ask if anyone can suggest a longer one. Write the suggestions on the board or on a white board, lined chart pad, or whatever modern technology has provided for you. It needs to be speedy and efficient. Students will not wait around politely for very long before wiggling.

As the suggested sentences get longer and longer, keep asking where the subject and verb are, and mark them with an oval over the subject

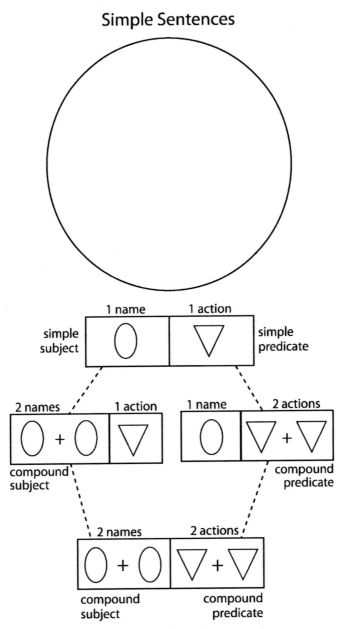

Figure 8.1. Simple sentences (a sorting pattern)

noun and the triangle over the verb. It is probably too much to expect that someone, in a zeal for competing and giving a truly long sentence, would suggest one with a compound subject or two action verbs the subject might be doing. Do not let that unsettle you. Just write it down, and draw two ovals, one over each of the two subjects; or draw two verb symbols over the two verbs in the case of a compound predicate. Be sure to rave about the student's sentence and ask if so-and-so has tricked the class. Can they figure out what they have in this latest sentence example?

Will someone ask you for the world's longest sentence in English? I hope not, although someone may have entered one in the *Guinness Book of Records* somewhere along the way. There is also the possibility that someone will offer a sentence with a verb phrase. Mark each verb with the verb triangle, but mention they are a phrase and they act as a single-word verb. You can get into the idea of how verbs can suggest time sense, that is, *verb tenses* later.

Now think about it. You have a class of students who have a definition of a complete sentence, and you have a concept model, a rectangle in two parts with an oval for a subject and a triangle for a verb. But someone has suggested a sentence where two subjects do the same action. Or perhaps someone stated a sentence where a single subject can do two different things. Draw the simple pattern with one oval and one triangle. Then ask the class how the sentence you just wrote for them to see is different. Yes, there are two subjects doing the action, or yes, the subject is doing two actions. Then ask, "How should we draw a sentence pattern if it has two subjects? What if it has two verbs?" Remind yourself, now, by looking back at figure 8.1.

With the four options from that sentence pattern in your mind, try drawing the initial pattern, then draw one of the changes—say the compound subject pattern below the subject side of the first simple pattern to show the subject was doubled. Ask, "What other changes could we make, or did we make?" You should get the answer, "We can double the verb. Just draw two verb symbols for a sentence subject to do." If you have the initial sentence, and the doubled subject below it to the left, you should put the example with the doubled verb to the right under the predicate side of the original example. It sounds like piling up blocks. You have two *bricks* on the bottom, and one brick topping them across the middle.

If you have drawn these quickly, you can ask if anyone sees another option. That question should get you the answer that you could have two subjects *and* two verbs. While you draw that possibility below the two patterns that are side by side, ask if anyone can make up a sentence that would be an example of one with two subjects and two predicates.

You have just developed that pattern for four kinds of simple sentences, which will also work for the term: a simple, independent clause. You could label the parts of each pattern with *simple subject* or *compound subject* if the class is mature enough to deal with such detail. Add *simple predicate* (verb) and *compound predicate* as labels on the corresponding pattern. If compound, as a term, is not a vocabulary word students have experience with, just stick to two—two subjects or two verbs. Students learn about compound words early in their school years—cowboy, farmhouse—so a connection might be made that way.

In the pattern above, the large circle stands for all the examples of simple sentences you can create in the English language, and they can all be sorted into one of the four examples. The brain is wired to identify, compare, and sort information about concepts. If you have prepared the Simple Sentence sorting pattern in advance, bring it out now. Have each student jot four sentences on a piece of scrap paper or a notebook page. Make each set fit the four variations you have on the chalkboard. When students are ready, whip out your prepared sorting pattern, and if you can project it and write on it also, fill in at least two examples students give for each of the four types. Write the samples in the large circle, number them, and then have students sort them by putting the sentence number by the appropriate pattern.

Sentences for Various Purposes

Remember that basic concept models represent something generic, and while sentences have a variety of forms, they also serve different purposes. Before sentence structure becomes more complicated, clear up the purposes idea. Aim for constructing a visual representation of the four kinds of sentences we use for various reasons: Declarative Statements, Questions, Commands or Polite Requests, and Exclamations. Collect a set of examples of each kind, and display or present them as a subset or a group. Establish that they are all complete sentences with subject, predicate, and appropriate punctuation, but there is something different about each set. That will lead to a second basic concept pattern, figure 8.2.a, a concept dimension pattern. They are seeing sentences, but four different kinds according to their purpose.

Kinds of Sentences (purpose)

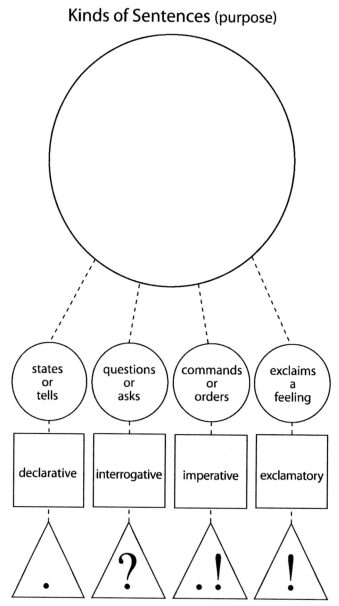

Figure 8.2.a.   Four kinds of sentences (purpose)

It should not take long to establish the four reasons for saying something in sentence form. Sets of statements and questions, commands, and excited expressions are probably efficient for all ages. You could set up a situation for younger children, telling them to imagine they are sitting at the breakfast table in the morning before leaving for school. What might your mother say? "What do you want for breakfast? Did you sleep well last night? What on earth were you dreaming when you were talking in your sleep?" Those were questions, and young children would know that already.

What might you answer her? "I feel like waffles. And I did sleep well. I don't remember talking in my sleep any time." Students know answers are just telling sentences. If you write any of these on the board, project them with a multimedia projector, or use your interactive white board, ask students how to show the difference between questions and answers when they are writing a story. That leads us to ending punctuation marks.

Tell the students to imagine that a sleepy person might dawdle, and then ask what might the mother say? "Get a move on. You'll be late for the bus." She would tell them to hurry. That is giving a command. Introduce levels of anxiety when commands are given: periods will do for general statements to do something, but if danger is involved, or a parent is angered by slow cooperation, students of all ages know that an exclamation point will let readers know the boiling point is approaching. The latter lets you point out that excited commands, and simple statements of excitement and emotion can both use exclamation points.

Figure 8.2a gave me an idea when I was preparing it. I had wanted to use the small circles to sort the kinds of sentences from the bottomless well into the right *buckets*, but I wanted to give my middle school students the proper labels for English class. I also wanted to get the punctuation marks appropriate to the purpose into the pattern some way. When I added the squares and triangles, what I saw made me think of those toddler toys, schoolhouse or garage or farm, with the little figures like Japanese *kokeishi* dolls from Sapporo—the "head on a stick" dolls. They were also like the corncob dolls pioneer families on the American Plains made for their daughters. I decided to make a second pattern, figure 8.2b, for reviewing. I turned the circles into heads.

Kinds of Sentences (purpose)

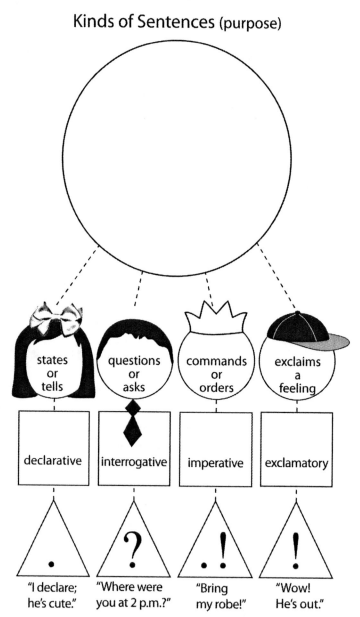

Figure 8.2.b.   Four kinds of sentences (purpose) review

Having lived in Tennessee and Virginia, I picked up on a *Scarlet O'Hara* stereotype. "Ah declayuh, he is the cutest man ah've evah seen." With a feminine hair-do complete with bow, and a reminder on the head, "states or tells," the label *declarative* picks up on the "Ah declayuh . . . ," the period is there, and the hinting sentence, "I declare; he's cute," finishes the mnemonic effect. The interrogative sentence was inspired by detective and lawyer shows on television where everyone knows, even young children, that the lawyer interrogates the witness. Use the verb *interrogates*, but the hint is a typical question: "Where were you at 2 A.M.?" Notice the lawyer has a conservative haircut and wears a shirt and tie.

I completed the review pattern with a crowned *emperor* who gives *imperial* commands or *imperatives*, as "Bring me my robe!" or "Off with her head!" but could just as easily say, "Prime Minister, my scepter, please." And everyone yells at a baseball game, "He's out!" That completed, with the umpire's baseball cap, the hints for the four kinds of sentences according to their purpose. It was safe to return to sentences and clauses with the groundwork established.

WHEN IT COMES TO SENTENCE STRUCTURE

When it comes to sentence structure, you have to ask the class if they have noticed that some sentences are long, some really long, and others shorter, even really short! You might mention that 150 years ago, authors wrote such long sentences that one might begin on the left hand page of the book and end on the right. That would be Charles Dickens and Henry James, for two. Ask them if such a sentence would be a run-on sentence that would be hard to understand, and see what they think.

Sentences and Fragments
(or Here Come Clauses—They Are Not for Everyone)

By sixth grade, students know about incomplete sentences and complete sentences, but they may not know why a group of words is one or the other. In general conversation, one speaker might state something and the other respond with a comment that is not a complete sentence, or it might be long enough to be a sentence, but the thought in isolation is not fully clear.

> First speaker: "I was downtown yesterday."
> Second speaker: "You went down in all that rain?"
> First speaker: "Why not?"
> Second speaker: "The rain, for one thing."
> First speaker: "Rain, drain, train . . . Why should the rain stop me?"
> Second speaker: "And you saw . . .?
> First speaker: "Yep! Right in the middle of the mall."

We cannot hear the inflection in this printed conversation, but we can read between the lines and guess that the second speaker knew the probable motivation behind the first speaker's going downtown in pouring rain. And with both speakers on the scene for the conversation, any vague information would bring forth a question from one person to clarify what the other was saying. We do not have that possibility on the printed page, not to mention electronic mailing programs, but then I overlook those animated smiley faces.

Sometimes, to introduce the idea of clauses, both independent and dependent, I would act out a phone conversation where the students heard only one side:

> Person on the phone: "Hi, it's Emily here." (greeting)
> "No, not at this moment . . ." (response to a question)
> "When he's through at his job, around 5 p.m." (second response)
> "About 5:30." (response)
> "I'll tell him you called, and will call back." (sign-off)

We would discuss this conversation in terms of what the caller probably said, and how you had to hear both sides to form complete statements with the fragmented answers. With a few more written examples or those displayed on an overhead projector or a student handout, we would arrive at the idea that some groups of sentences had subjects and predicates but were not complete thoughts. You needed more information. You had to pause and think what the fragment might mean.

At this point, in teaching cognitively, I would refer to the basic sentence pattern, but draw it as a parallelogram. It was a *leaning sentence*.

That is, it needed a complete sentence to lean on, as a person with a broken leg needed a crutch to lean on. Indeed, one year, one of my students nicknamed dependent clauses "broken-legged clauses." We drew the patterns and added the labels: independent clause and dependent clause.

If you know that cute play on words about clauses and pauses, you could throw it in now for older students:

> . . . "What's the difference between a clause and a cat?"
> "There's a comma for the pause at the end of a clause, but cats have claws at the ends of their paws."

I think of Edward Lear and Ogden Nash when I run into such wordplay, but my quotation sources do not seem to be of help this time. Herein the author is unknown.

Elliptical Sentences

In the early twenty-first century, we are seeing repeatedly what my teachers and my colleagues have taught as incomplete sentences. They look like sentences, they are punctuated as sentences, and sometimes they even have a subject and the verb in the predicate, but they are not a complete thought. They could be if you reworded them slightly and punctuated them with question marks, the ones that start with who, what, or when, anyway.

> "When we are going downtown . . . " could become
> "When are we going downtown?"

Ask up-to-date freelance editors, and I count a couple in my circle of friends, and they will tell you these are called *elliptical sentences*. It is a new way of punctuating and writing that takes into account oral speech.

When I did my research for my dissertation on how middle school students' writing changes (George Mason University, 1996), I hypothesized that fragments punctuated as sentences happened with my eighth graders because the students had the mature oral style for writing more complicated sentences, but did not have the sophisticated knowledge of how to punctuate them. They separated the main clause from a dependent one in what was actually a complex sentence. I only wonder if teachers in public school systems are actually presenting the elliptical sentence or just mentioning them in an aside. How many student readers notice them in books or just accept them?

Imagine my shock at looking in my old college handbooks and finding the term elliptical as referring to sentences understood because the words omitted could be filled in by the reader. I guess, not only does language change, but so do definitions and usage. I remember, and I am sure you do too, when *bad* was a negative judgment, but a quarter century later, it was a compliment. A similar reversal involved the word *raunchy*.

For review: We have a pattern for four kinds of sentences that we speak depending on the reason for speaking—to declare something, to ask something, to give a direction or command, and to exclaim something with emotion. We also have a pattern for simple sentences to demonstrate the two parts that make them up, and how each part, subjects or predicates, can be simple or compound in four possible combinations. Now we can add the idea of clauses to introduce to older students who might be ready for more abstract thinking. Clauses make possible the dimensions of sentence structure. How many ways can we combine independent and dependent clauses in the same sentence? We might need algebra for a numerical answer. We just answer elliptically: "Lots!"

One academic year, I was at the blackboard, a real slate blackboard, and using the letters I and D for Independent and Dependent. It must have been income tax time, because thinking of the term *dependent* made me think of children as tax deductions. Suddenly, I was inspired to create The Marital Law of Sentence Structure. As I look back on this episode, I wonder that I did not end up with parents pounding the door or going straight to the principal to complain. I was working with sixth or seventh graders in the last decade of my career, and nothing I said in class was any worse than the children saw on television, which may explain why my remarks made not a ripple on the surface of life in the classroom. But was it questionable, possibly even in poor taste?

Sixth graders know the word compound from learning compound words like *cowboy* and *nightgown* in spelling lessons. *Compound word* was easily related to combining two independent clauses to make a *compound sentence*. I began printing the letters in an arithmetical style on the board: I + I = C (Compound Sentence). Then I got to the: I + D = Cx (Complex Sentence). The light bulb turned on, and I told the story that follows.

Two young independent clauses go to a restaurant or meet at a party, and if they like each other, they may get together often and decide they really like each other. If they do enjoy each other's company, they may decide to get married to compound their happiness: I + I = C. It is possible that, if they decide they have enough love to share, they will plan to have a family, even though that means added responsibility, and life becomes more complicated. That was written as I + I + D (a little dependent clause) = C-Cx. I may even have remarked that little dependents sometimes bring the necessity for a diaper-pail in the nursery or a way to take care of disposable diapers. Diapers and dependent both start with D. I probably did not have time to deal with the recycling problem.

The story continues: But we all know that, sometimes, independent people are not as responsible as they should be, and sometimes mothers have to raise their children without the help of fathers. Then life is really complicated, really complex. Printed out, this resulted in I + D = Cx (Complex). "Hindsight [being] better than foresight," I would say *single parents* now, and not dump it all on the mothers. Reality changes.

But you are probably shaking your head in disbelief. If you could never pull this off in front of twelve-year-olds, do not worry. Stick with broken-leg clauses, or *leaning* clauses, or clauses that need a crutch to help them stand alone, to make complete sense. High school students would have too much information to bring to this story-explanation, and you might have them rolling on the floor. Check your audience before saying anything. These are freer times, if not more open times than when I was in sixth grade, but schools have to maintain standards. Let us return to the topic with figure 8.3.

Practice in Finding and Writing Different Sentence Structures

Since the sentence-structure favored by a writer or an author is one part, one element, of an author's *style* of writing, it might be interesting to send students on a scavenger hunt for sentences in an assigned story

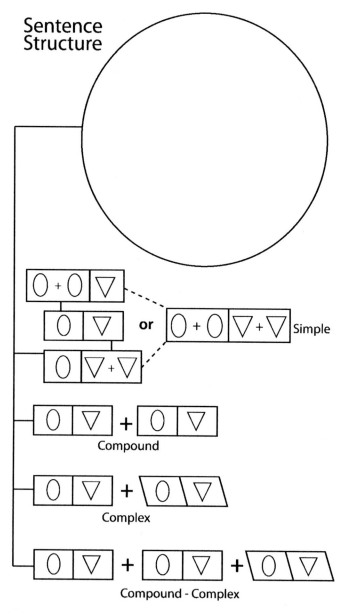

Figure 8.3. Four kinds of sentences (structure)

or in the book they are reading for the next book report, or—and this could be fun in more ways than one—have them read children's books aloud to the class so fellow students can to try to spot the different sentence types as they hear them. You can then send the students to read to lower grade children. Everyone benefits with that project.

Class practice can also involve writing sentences according to a pattern of sentence structure, or teachers can have students analyze a piece of their own writing to find how varied their sentences are. Did they use all or mostly simple sentences? Did they include a few longer sentences too? How many were compound sentences, but how many included both dependent and independent clauses?

HOW MUCH GRAMMAR TO COVER?

Sixth Grade Grammar

When I was teaching identified gifted students in that three-year program, in the sixth grade, we covered the basics:

1. Rediscovered the eight parts of speech, which was an assumption on my part
2. Reviewed the four kinds of sentences depending on purpose
3. Contemplated four kinds of sentences depending on structure
4. Involved the concept of clauses: independent and dependent

We dived into clause patterns, too. Simple sentences could have subject and verb, but the verb could be an action (transitive) or being (intransitive) verb.

Teachers have a good chance to spur vocabulary habits at this point. Students of all levels can be introduced to the idea of some words being very old, even from languages not spoken regularly today; parts of those words have meanings, not just the words themselves. *Trans* means across, so with action verbs, we call them *transitive* verbs if they transfer, or send across, the verb's action to a person or object. Do take time to list a few words students can suggest that have *trans* as a syllable in them. Is the meaning *across* consistent in these?

We took on sentences with action verbs that had *object complements:* indirect and direct objects, or just direct objects. They complete the idea of the verb's action. Making things visual in grammar usually clears up the indirect object problem quickly.

You have marked the verb and determined it is an action verb, and you probably have put those noun-ovals over all the nouns in the sentence and determined which was the subject-noun. But, what about those nouns in the predicate? A noun receiving the action of the verb is the *direct object*.

"Tom Sawyer carried a paintbrush" (see figure 8.3a).

With an indirect object, there will be at least two nouns. Start an arrow at the right side of the verb symbol and ask which noun received the action? You can *not* draw a straight action line from the verb to the noun receiving the action, the direct object. You have to take an *indirect route* and go *around* the noun-oval that gets in the way. That shows you have an *in*direct object too. If prepositional phrases have already been dealt with, you can test the indirect object. See if you can place a *to* in front of it to make a prepositional phrase and then move that phrase to the end of the sentence.

"Tom Sawyer gave Huckleberry Finn the paintbrush" (see figure 8.3b).

The action verb is *gave*. Tom did the giving, so he is the subject. What did Tom give? He did not give Huckleberry Finn to anyone. He gave the paintbrush. The brush is the direct object. To emphasize this point, act out handing someone the paintbrush.

Huckleberry is named before the brush in the sentence. Huck is the indirect object.

Test: "Tom Sawyer gave the paintbrush *to* Huckleberry Finn."

And linking verbs (intransitive—they do not have an action to transfer because *in* means not) have their complements, the *subject complements,* called *predicate nouns* or *predicate adjectives*. Subject complements complete the idea of the subject. You can put an equal sign inside the verb symbol to show, as in a math equation, the noun in the predicate identifies, or names in another way, the noun subject.

"Huck Finn *was* a reluctant painter" (see figure 8.3c).

Was is not an action verb. It has no action to transfer. Who was Huck Finn? He was a *painter* in this situation. *Painter* is the predicate nominative or predicate noun, the subject complement for Huck Finn. It identifies, or names, Huck as a painter. If you said: "Huck Finn was talented" (see figure 8.3d.), you would have a predicate adjective, an adjective in the predicate that described the subject.

Practice Sentences for Object Complements

It is a good thing to make up your own practice sentences every now and then. You put in what you want students to notice and remember

Direct Object
Transitive Verb (action)

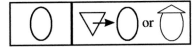

Figure 8.3.a.   Direct object pattern

Indirect Object (no "to")
Transitive (action) Verb

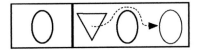

Figure 8.3.b.   Indirect object pattern

Predicate Noun
Predicate Pronoun
Intransitive linking Verb

Figure 8.3.c.   Predicate noun

Predicate Adjective
Intransitive, Linking Verb

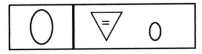

Figure 8.3.d.   Predicate adjective pattern

Figure 8.3.a, b, c, d.   Example patterns for complements

and leave out extraneous details that might be distractions. The sentences given here make a good handout, transparency, or projected exercise for the interactive white board. They are short and directly to the point. It is easy to draw sentence rectangles and use the noun-ovals and the verb-triangles to illustrate them visually.

There are two kinds of object complements; notice the *e* as in *complete*. Put the following sentences on the board as examples of direct objects:

> Jonathan ate the apple.
> The apple had a worm.
> The worm had made a hole.
> Jonathan didn't see it.
> He ate the whole thing.

Put the following sentences on the board as examples of indirect objects:

> Susie gave Jonathan the apple.
> She'd have given me the worm.
> Jonathan will give her a piece of his mind!

There are two kinds of subject complements.

Put the following sentences on the board as examples of predicate nouns:

Actually the worm was protein.
Worms are food, really.
Jonathan's apple was a Macintosh.
The worm must have been a bachelor.
The hole was his home. The hole was *it*.

Put the following sentences on the board as examples of predicate adjectives:

The apple was good.
The worm must have been delicious, too.
The hole was probably tasteless.
Was this snack nutritious? (This snack *was* nutritious.)
Jonathan was very hungry.

We kept the definitions simple: A predicate noun was a noun in the predicate that named the subject in another way. A predicate adjective was an adjective in the predicate that described the subject.

Figure 8.4 includes both the sentences about Jonathan and the worm in the apple, as well as the concept models for each clause pattern. Limited time or the need for efficiency may determine whether you use one approach or the other, or a combination.

And Now for a Bit of Diagramming

With the clause patterns, I threw in some basic diagramming. On the blackboard, the rectangle with the two sections became the sentence line with the dividing vertical line between subject and predicate. I erased the ends and top of the sentence rectangle to begin with, and extended the dividing line below the sentence line.

Diagramming cleared up prepositional phrases for some. And the line dividing the verb from the rest of the sentence really helped when a linking verb required drawing the line after the verb and showing it leaning back towards the subject. Take a look at figure 8.5. I would even extend the line as a dashed line, forming an arc back toward the subject, and I would add a V-point for the arrowhead, too. Every little reminder helps with abstract notions.

Sentences with Complements ("completers")

Two Kinds of Object Complements:

Jonathan ate the apple.

The apple had a worm.

The worm had made a hole.

Jonathan didn't see it.

He ate the whole thing.

Direct Object
Transitive Verb (action)

Susie gave Jonathan the apple.

She'd have given me the worm.

Jonathan will give her a
piece of his mind!

Indirect Object (no "to")
Transitive (action) Verb

Two Kinds of Object Complements:

Actually, the worm was protein.

Worms are good, really.

Jonathan apple was a Macintosh.

The worm must have been a
bachelor.

The hole was his home. The hole
was it.

Predicate Noun
Predicate Pronoun
Intransitive linking Verb

The apple was good.

The worm must have been
delicious too.

The hole was probably tasteless.

Was this snack nutritious? (This
snack was nutritious.)

Jonathan was very hungry.

Predicate Adjective
Intransitive, Linking Verb

Figure 8.4.   Sentence complements handout

Diagramming

Diagramming maps out how words in a sentence relate to one another.

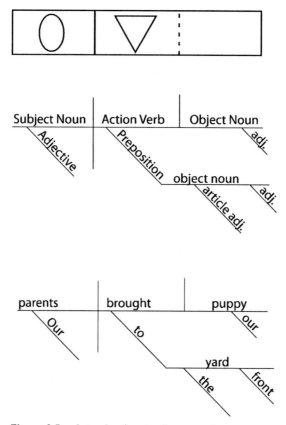

Figure 8.5.   Introduction to diagramming

Seventh Grade Grammar   Remember, at this point I had the same students from sixth grade in seventh grade the following year. In the seventh grade, after a review of parts of speech and clause patterns:

1. I acknowledged that we could do more than just placing a prepositional phrase under the word on the sentence line that it de-

scribed (verb or noun). We could actually distinguish them as being adverbial or adjectival prepositional phrases. (The students got a kick out of the long-i in adjectival. I learned that from a Latin teacher colleague.)

2. We continued using diagramming and hit sentence complements a little harder.

3. And we had an introduction to the idea that dependent clauses could act as parts of speech, and, therefore, we had noun clauses, adjective clauses, and adverb clauses.

Eighth Grade Grammar This was my third year with the same group. I cannot recommend strongly enough continuing with a class for more than one year, but that is a philosophical subject I would preach or lecture about any time at all. Right now, the topic is grammar.

With all that happens in the eighth grade, we still made time for grammar. After all, next year the students entered high school in a pre-college program with foreign languages and advanced English literature courses. High school teachers have expectations. After a review of the parts of speech, clauses, and clause patterns:

1. We learned to diagram compound and complex sentences, and how to show the relationships between multiple clauses diagrammed for the same sentence. (Hint: For one form of practice, I gave blank diagrams to fill in with forms provided for compound and complex sentences, but I made sure several sentences had the same number of words so students had to think before filling the words in on the diagrams.)

2. The English teachers' term for dependent clauses—subordinate clause—was introduced so that it did not sound too strange when upper level English teachers used it for our "broken-legged clauses."

You have another vocabulary side-trip to take here. *Subordinate* is not a vocabulary word many students use regularly, although if a parent runs an office in a business, the students may have heard about the *subordinates* under their management. Pull the word apart and point out *sub* meaning under (as in *submarine*, under the sea), and point out the *ord*, which is like the word *order*. Subordinate clauses are under or lesser in importance than the main or independent clauses they need for support. Use the same approach if your class is ready for the term subordinating conjunctions, the joining words that make a clause dependent.

3. We spent time on verbals: infinitives, gerunds, and participles.
4. And last, we took a cursory look at verb conjugation.

We do not sit around in English classes saying, "I love, you love, he, she, or it loves . . ." the way we learn to conjugate a tense in Latin, "*amo, amas, amat . . .*" or another foreign language. But I wanted to cover the possibility that the term might turn up. (Small groups tackled select verbs for this goal. Did I risk my reputation and allow them to select their own verbs? I do not recall, but since I cannot remember, probably no *iffy* verbs were chosen.)

Was I afraid the younger high school teachers would not use terms like subjunctive and imperative for moods, and regular, progressive, and emphatic for verb tense forms? What about regular, present perfect, and past perfect tenses? These were *my kids*, and I wanted them to be ready for everything. I also believed in exposure. If I exposed them to verb conjugations, and later in their schooling, if the subject came up, a little spark of memory might bounce around and remind them of what they had seen once before. For older and wiser teens, the memory might make more sense then.

A term we once had for the basic sentence—the sentence skeleton—was replaced, some twenty-five years ago, by a *kernel* sentence when sentence-combining was a strategy to lead students to write longer or more varied sentences. It works well with all levels of student learning. It develops a sense, or at least an awareness, of style. That original sentence pattern, the rectangle with the two parts, gets you started.

Gauchos ride. (subject and verb)
Their horses are swift.
Their horses are strong.
They streak across the *Pampas*.
The Pampas is an area in Argentina.

Older students should easily create sentences like:

The *gauchos* ride across the Pampas of Argentina on swift, strong horses.
Streaking across the Pampas of Argentina are the *gauchos*, riding their swift, strong horses.

When you look at the results of the students' work, you can use the symbols to quickly locate the original bits of the given kernels before they were combined.

What Else Is There?

Teachers can do a great deal with grammar and can spend a great deal of time on it, but it is worth it. If you just straighten up some English usage problems with good reason, it is a start on correcting what some people see as our language's steady decline.

Take *I* and *me*, for example. So many times a student would come up to me and ask, "Can me and Susie go to the library?" Sometimes it was, "Can Susie and me go to the library." Either way, there was a serious problem there. I held to correcting the can-or-may rule of physically able versus having permission. If I student approached me with, "Can I go to the library?" I would ask them quizzically, "How do you feel?" Then the confusion was theirs, and I could continue with, "Do you have a fever, a headache, do you have the strength to get there and back?" That was all that was needed for them to self-correct with, "May I go?"

But the use of the objective pronoun, *me,* as a sentence subject, was an assault on my ears. My standard response was, "Me go to the library?" I sounded like a two or three-year-old. Fortunately, students also heard it that way, but from an adult, a teacher. In sixth grade, they usually corrected themselves in that instance, too, but sometimes I would supply the correct wording. If the students know clause patterns, however, they know why there is a difference in subject and object (nominative and objective) pronouns.

In one class group, I had a student who heard me frequently correcting students—I trust in a kindly and smiling fashion—and said, "*Me* doesn't do anything; *I* do everything." She had made that observation. When I displayed a poster board with her reminder, I worded it, "*Me* doesn't do anything; the *I* does everything." The "I does" stops you when you hear it. But in conversation with a student, I would chide, "*Me* doesn't do anything." The way students heard that coming from their teacher, responding with a pause and a grin as the light came on, I knew it was effective.

Before I bring this chapter to a close, I must recommend a series of ancient texts that will not require a paleo-linguist's skills of translation. If you can find, in a used bookstore or via the Internet, a secondary school copy of the Harcourt Brace Javanovich English series, *English Grammar and Composition*, the copyright dates for which go back to 1958, you will have a solid friend to consult when questions arise in diagramming sentences. Sometimes lovingly referred to as Warriner's, and then derisively when people rolled their eyes at the idea of traditional grammar teaching, it has chapters on the parts of speech, phrases, and clauses with clear diagrams and straight-forward definitions. You cannot lose. I rescued my Warriner's *Fifth Course* (1973) from the trash and cherish it still.

A Final Word

Remind your students of the economic value of good grammar, as in correct Standard English, when they apply for jobs in their adult life and are interviewed. Tell them that stating, "Me and my friend are hoping to work in the same business" is not going to win them any extra points on the hiring scale, even if they want to suggest their strong interest in the position. It is important to know when Standard English is required even if, at home or with friends, they lapse into the colloquial. Students need to feel that making the effort in how they say things will be worth it to their future. The first impression is one of sight, but it is followed quickly by one of hearing. Eventually, "Actions speak louder than words."

A Pertinent and Coincidental Quote

In the *Parade* section of the *Washington Post* for Sunday, September 24, 2006, there was a question about grammar in the "Ask Marilyn" column on page 26. "My students increasingly question the value of learning basic grammar. They say that, in the future, computers will correct their mistakes automatically. What would you tell them?—Name withheld, Sanford, Maine."

Marilyn vos Savant replied: "Even if computers could discern what students wanted to say (despite their errors), students must learn not only basic grammar but also sophisticated and highly complex grammar. Otherwise, the students won't be able to comprehend what they read to the fullest extent. Almost as important, they won't realize their limitations."

To this I say, "Amen."

9

WHAT ABOUT MATH AND SCIENCE?
THIS ONE'S SHORT AND SWEET

Up to this point, the book has obviously displayed what might seem like a bias toward language and cultures—English and social studies. Three quarters of my teaching career focused on those two subjects and only one-fourth on all subjects, including art and music, in self-contained classrooms. But when teaching in a team of four or a team of two, I was definitely *exposed* to math and science, and even correlated and integrated topic and unit areas with science at least, if at an oblique angle with mathematics on occasion. (Palindromes are a nice bridge between English and math.) When I was teaching science and math myself, I developed all sorts of visual ways to help students comprehend what had also required some effort on my part at their age. Still, there are other reasons why mathematics and science seem to have received short shrift in this tome.

Essentially, these two curricular areas have visual representations, concept patterns, of their own. In fact, when clarifying the meaning of a basic concept in the first of her course sequences, Dr. Fulton referred to the posters we often see in science classrooms, posters of birds or flowers. They show a prototype bird (beak, wings, tail, feathers, claws on legs, eyes) or flower (corolla, sepals, petals, anther, pistil, stem, root system, pollen), and label all the parts that help biologists define them as such, but unless some Amazonian researcher has spotted a heretofore unknown species illustrated on the posters, they are no bird or flower you have ever seen.

Just stop and recall your general science classes. Can you recall any elementary science lessons? Were there posters of, or did you draw and label cross-sections of, a volcano or the layers in a geological cross-section of a mountain or a canyon? What about that poster that represented the Water Cycle?

I do not know about you, but I can still see the sloping land on the left side of the poster, or it might have been the science book illustration (See end of Note 5 for Chapter 7). Clouds were dropping rain over the mountains; rain was collecting in woodland streams and emptying into a river running down to the lakeside or ocean's beach. There at the water's edge, the sun was out and drying up the rain (remember the "Itsy-bitsy Spider"), so the clouds could collect the evaporated moisture again and, when there was enough, drop it on the land where it would run down the slope in streams and rivers to the sea, and evaporate and rise up to be caught on dust particles in clouds, until the clouds got too heavy, and it rained, and . . . and . . . and . . . (no, you do not have to diagram that run-on sentence.)

SCIENCE POSSIBILITIES

Just grab a science textbook and thumb through the chapters. Where social studies books had timelines, maps, photos and drawings, graphs (oops! we did not mention graphs, but we do here), and charts, and maybe a cross-section or two of homes in different cultures, science has cross-sections and drawings, circuits, and ways to show systems and cycles. The list of topics seems endless when you are planning lessons for the year's overview, all of which have their own visuals.

Science Can Use Event Frames, Too

I suppose you could teach very successfully without worrying about basic concept patterns in math and science because of their natural propensity for calling on a teacher's illustrating methods, labeled posters, and bulletin boards, even three-dimensional models in science in particular. But there are concept patterns we have already considered that can be applied very efficiently here.

The *event frame* itself, or the *procedure frame* variation, can be employed when summarizing events in science. A frame could show the way Alexander Fleming discovered penicillin in the mid-twentieth-century, or Archimedes weighed the crown of Hiero, the King of Syracuse, back in the time of ancient Greece. Study the following cycle pattern using two event frames as shown in figure 9.1.

The Water Cycle could be presented in two event frames: a frame of boxes starting with rain that forms streams flowing to the sea. The second frame below is reversed: water evaporates in sunlight and heat, fills the clouds with moisture, is blown over the land, and falls like rain. Put an arrow connecting the end box of the first frame with the last box of the second one, but remember—that box is the first step of the reversal of the process, picking up with the evaporation of the oceans and lakes and proceeding to where the clouds are forming and dropping rain again. Connect that box with an arrow to the first box of the top event frame. The arrows connect the frames and show the repetition of the Water Cycle, which is not unlike the event frame demonstrating the cycle of the Nile River in Egypt. Remember figure 3.6 in the chapter on the Event Frame?

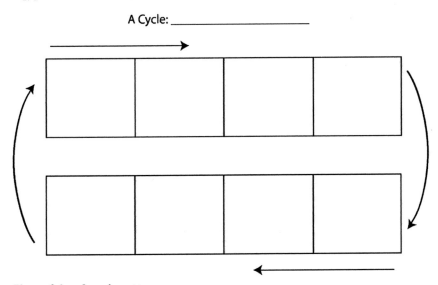

Figure 9.1. A cycle pattern

Goofy ABLGUF Works Here, Too

The six dimensions of a complete description, nicknamed ABLGUF, from chapter two is very helpful for science topics. Students write reports and give speeches about myriads of things, systems, or processes. These describe what the things or systems are, what they look like, how they work, what they produce, what you call them, where you find them, and what effects they have on their surroundings or the people who use them. Students compete to create new inventions and then have to explain and demonstrate them clearly to others. A science series on television used to follow a single invention from its inception to its influence on life, and its eventual metamorphoses into modern items we use. ABLGUF can be used along a time line to trace such evolving of inventions in a physics or energy unit.

Models can be built to demonstrate other things and situations: how a canal lock works, how water flows to seek its level, and how volcanoes erupt. You just have to imagine Science Fairs you have visited to think of things to visually represent and then clearly and completely describe.

I want to include something here that is part model and part visual representation or pattern, and certainly a concept that sometimes defies the imagination: our solar system.

I was in fourth or fifth grade of elementary school, and we were studying the planets. I decided to draw a picture of the planets in their orbits and color the poster because I just loved drawing and coloring. My father was a wonderful mathematician and worked in a bank, calculating totals in his mind, faster than the hand-cranked adding machines of the times. I went to him for help with how far apart to draw the circles for each planet. I had the sizes of the planets figured out by enlarging them from the textbook chart. I do not need to tell you that we could either represent the relative sizes of the planets, or the relative distances between them, not both, on the same poster board!

But, when I was teaching in Tehran at the American Community School some decades back, a college friend there at the same time worked out a solution to this problem. He figured out the size of the various planets and found balls in toy shops of the various sizes he needed, but the smallest planets he made with solder on the heads of pins or something equally slender and supporting. Then, he calculated the distances in feet to miles, or meters to kilometers, or possibly both. He took his class out on the steps of the school's main entrance and was able to have students stand on the steps and across the playground to the main gate, holding the appropriate planet models approximating distances between the first three planets.

But then, he was forced to tell the students and show them on a city map of Tehran, where the other planets would be located from the school gate and up through the northern part of the city to some foothill suburbs and villages at the Alborz Mountain Range. He made his point! When translated to their own familiar stomping grounds, imagining the huge distances while looking at the relatively scaled planet models was more than simply effective. It was, as they used to say, "Awesome!"

My mother raised us with adages like, "Honest confession is good for the soul." I must confess here to learning something appallingly late in my career. I had an "Aha!" moment in two areas of my life at the same time. I had either read or had seen in one of PBS television's series on the brain that research had been done on how well students understand and retain information. They tested college students on how much they really understood from their high school science classes about the universe and particularly about our solar system. Their confusions and misremembering or misunderstandings were pervasive.

I sympathized, but then it came to me to discuss the seasons in a social studies class of sixth graders when I was in my late thirties. The idea of the Northern Hemisphere's having winter when the Southern Hemisphere had summer was not clear to some of my eleven- and twelve-year-olds. Teachers in my mother's day might have used a candle or a flashlight, and a globe. I stood up next to my overhead projector desk and held my pencil at an angle representative of the earth's axis. As I moved it in an orbit around the projector's light representing the sun, I kept the pencil steady to prove that at times the Northern Hemisphere was farther from the sun than the southern. And then, something clicked.

At the same time that I was thinking, in the back of my mind, about those confused college students, I realized that I had gone through my life, to that point, thinking and saying, "During summer, the earth is tipped toward the sun . . ." I was keeping in my mind an erroneous fact, an untruth! The earth did not *tip* back and forth on its axis; it remained steady. Its position in its orbit about the sun explained the nearness or distance of the hemispheres from the sun in creating the seasons! I think I remember being so shocked at my years of possibly dealing out misinformation about the solar system, that I told my class on the spot. After all, I wanted students to know even adults made mistakes, and it was better if they realized it and even became cynical enough to question their teachers—politely. I also hoped they noticed the fact that adults could keep learning.

What I did not really figure out was whether I had not had enough information from the science book illustration of the seasons on earth to understand correctly or whether it was someone's use of the verb, tipped, that miscued me. Providing enough information when building important concepts for students is crucial, or their frontal lobes will choose a way to remember that makes sense for them.

Of course, science has its mnemonics, too, feeding into the brain's penchant for novelty and play with language. You can be reminded of the order of the planets from the sun by noting the first letters of the words in the following statement: Meek violet terrestrials make just such unusual new pets. That gem was found in Michele B. Slung's *The Absent-Minded Professor's Memory Book* (1985, p. 51), along with "Roy G. Biv," the colors of light as bent into a rainbow by a prism—red, orange, yellow, green, blue, indigo, and violet. You can just imagine what other tidbits can be discovered therein.

MATH POSSIBILITIES

The event frame also serves the field of mathematics. Any event that was important to mathematical discoveries can be shown in its steps toward the eventual conclusion: an image of engineers in ancient Egypt measuring the height of the pyramids with basic geometry comes to my mind, but there is my interest in geography and cultures rearing its head again.

Dr. Fulton used procedure frames to lay out the steps of an arithmetical skill, such as addition or multiplication, frame by frame, with examples labeled within the frames and a caption telling what to do at that point. If the title of a lesson is two-digit (place) addition with regrouping, the teacher might need a three-frame chart (see figure 9.2).

Two-Digit Addition with Regrouping		
Add the ones: 13 = 1 ten 3 ones	Regroup: Add the ten to the ten's place.	Add the tens:
84 +19 3	1 84 +19 3	1 84 +19 103

Figure 9.2. Two-digit addition with regrouping (Developmental Skills Institute)

The first step would show the problem and have the direction, "Add the ones." If the problem involved adding eighty-four and nineteen, the problem would be set up and a three shown in the sum in one's place. The sentence would read "13 = one ten and three ones." The second step would show the ten added to the tens' column above the eight from eighty-four and the one from the nineteen. The caption would say "Regroup: Add the ten to the tens' column." In the third frame or step, the direction would read, "Add the tens." And the final answer or sum would be completed (Fulton, 1986, 6).

Early grade teachers use pictures for addition and subtraction processes. The old-fashioned flannel board illustrates subtraction well: "Five little felt ducks waddling in a row," take away one or two and see how many are left. I see flannel board sets in toy stores, but I do not know if teachers still make use of their adaptability. I wager that approach goes back to Mesopotamia and scratching on damp clay tablets.

Mathematics also has that simple wonder, the number line, with which the place-value system is taught. Make a large poster board number-line, one with a decimal point obviously drawn in the middle, and the numerals moving away, place by place, to the right and the left. It is not a bad idea to color the places so that the hundredth's place to the right and the hundreds' place to the left of the decimal have the same color background for the numeral you are placing there. Of course, you will remember that introducing decimals is easier if you start with our monetary system. Most children learn to read prices early in the primary grades and, nowadays even earlier, I would imagine. The dollars are the numbers to the left of the *dot* and the numbers on the right are cents. You have to have a hundred cents or pennies to have a dollar. Piggy banks to the fore!

Cuisenaire Rods are available as commercially produced for use in schools and are found in stores that cater to parents interested in fostering their children's learning. These sets of cubes and rods in designated colors are manipulatives that allow students to line up ten cubes and substitute a ten-rod for them. It helps them understand grouping and regrouping in the base-tens system we use in decimals and whole numbers, and in working out basic arithmetic problems. If you are budget-starved, you just need to buy popsicles and save the sticks, wash them, and use them to count and bundle by tens. In Beirut, we used pistachio shells for unit-counters. You got to eat the luscious nutmeats first. What a deal!

I am sure teachers are still using concrete items to teach multiplication. The teacher has fifteen spools of thread and asks how many groups of three can be made. That leads to the idea of an arithmetic sentence that says, $5 \times 3 = 15$, once students have the idea that there are five groups of three spools each. The reverse is also true—you can find five groups of three spools in each group if you start with fifteen spools of thread. And there is the division statement: $15 \div 3$ (items per group or value of each group) is 5. Use actual objects, draw on the blackboard, give students handout sheets to draw their own groups, use the flannel board, and the concrete will be *seen* in the mind and eventually translate into the symbols with which we write out our findings.

But, novelty and your own two hands can catch the attention of young minds and give them a memorable experience with the nine-times multiplication table. I was in my second decade of teaching, and the instructor of a methods and materials course for elementary education majors at what was then Beirut College for Women in Lebanon. One of my Palestinian students shared a clever trick to help with the multiplication table for the numeral nine.

If you are multiplying 9 × 2, for example, you put out your two hands, side by side, thumbs together, fingers flat so all ten (thumbs count) are seen easily. Then you fold under the second finger from the left, the ring-finger on your left hand, which represents the number two, and the fingers still extended are the finger for number one on the left, and eight other fingers to the right of the number-two finger folded-down. *Voilá!* You have one and eight, or eighteen!

Now you try 9 × 5. Which finger on your left hand folds under for the five? Right! Your thumb is folded under. To your left you see four fingers, and on the right hand all five fingers are extended. Multiply 9 × 5 and you get 45. Now, why did none of my teachers know about that one when my father was drilling the times tables into my head? I stared at the dining room buffet doors for hours when I was in fourth grade. It does not matter, does it? It is just a clever trick, and it works. Now, how could we deal with those other times-tables? Do not ask me.

No, actually you could ask me. I learned that my mother-in-law drilled my husband, as a child, with a clock face. She drew it on a sheet of paper, put the numerals for the hours in their usual places, and the number by which they were multiplying in the center. This routine is neat because you point or touch the number you wrote in the middle. For eight, you state, "Eight times" and touch a number on the outer rim that you will multiply: three? "Eight times three is . . . " and give the answer. When a child or student can practice this exercise to the point of sing-song-ing it in rhythm as you bounce about the clock-hours, you know something has become automatic. Of course, they may have to sing-song the times-table during a math test to be sure of what they remember, but perhaps they can be encouraged to do it silently.

AND THERE YOU HAVE IT

Concepts in science are well illustrated, and having students draw examples of their own and label the parts of a volcano erupting, or the geological layers in a natural fault, or build the models themselves works beautifully. Mathematics has concepts that are more abstract, and creative teachers find ways to lead their students to necessary understandings, starting with concrete objects to introduce counting, with addition and subtraction before introducing multiplication and division. As things get farther and farther away from the concrete, relying on steps in a procedure frame helps students learn the way to find the sum, the difference, the product, or quotient when the numbers involved can not be counted on the fingers or figured out in some manipulative manner.

I will avoid commenting on mathematical classes involving algebra, trigonometry, and calculus. Those with training at higher levels probably have developed their own conceptual approaches. Bless them!

EPILOGUE
YOU'LL ADAPT IN YOUR OWN WAY

The late Senator Patrick Moynihan from New York State happened to write a column in a weekly news magazine in the early 1990s to point out how we change our daily language to make that which was perceived as wrong or negative, more acceptable, or at least tolerable. He had several examples, but alas, I only recall one, and that one probably because my generation was the *before* and current terminology is the *after*.

He offered *unwed mother*, which was used in the 1940s and 1950s, and when the situation of babies being *born out of wedlock* seemed to happen increasingly in the 1960s and on, *single mother* was deemed a more tolerable and less judgmental label. Thus, linguists study languages as spoken today and note changes, shifts, or additions from the past, noting also what probably caused them. I remember the column vividly, but never thought—fifteen years ago or more—to make a note of the source for a future footnote.

In a similar way, our linguistic expressions hint at an understanding that our brains store memories in visual ways, images of actual things, places, times, even abstract ideas. Say the word "justice," and your mind might conjure up a vision of the scales that must balance or even the sculpture atop the dome of the Supreme Court Building in Washington, D.C.—the female blind-folded Justice holding the balance scales of fairness.

Here are some remarks that usually suggest how our brains are *not* working:

Out of sight, out of mind.
Where are my keys? I'm trying to picture where I saw them last.
I'd better stop and do that before I forget.

Having studied for a test, when I could not bring up the answer in my mind, I could often remember where it was on the page in the text—upper left, lower right, under a picture—and then I would complain that I knew where it was, but I could not see it well enough to read it to find what I needed.

As teachers and parents, we need to be sure our students are learning the foundation tools that will serve them through their school years and their adult lives. Early concepts serve as initial anchors on which to attach further knowledge and language terms. If the brain stores much information from the senses in visual form, we can help in presenting information we deem necessary to their education through examples they will meet from day to day. Then, we can show them an image, a model of what they understand the concept to be.

Visual learners abound in our culture. Even before the bombardment of visual information through media and technology, we drew pictures to help our understanding. I cannot think of how many times I drew pictures to understand a story problem in arithmetic class. Nor can I even put a total number on the many illustrations I drew on the chalkboard or the overhead projector to help a class or a few students understand something I had said, or to which I had referred, or about which we were reading.

Cookbooks now come as video tapes and DVDs, and the same goes for home repairing and training videos in the personnel departments of the workplace. Exercise gurus lead us through activities for our cardiac, skeletal, and mental health on tapes or DVDs that we can put in our players and watch on the television screen. At a women's workout location I have frequented, there is a poster with a dozen illustrations of stretching positions for the warm-down after exercising. After seeing it for almost two years now, I could do the stretches at home by just remembering the chart. And how would I remember the chart? I would picture or visualize it.

As television recording devices allow viewers to fast-forward through commercials that break up the usual telecast programs, researchers are checking to see if commercials are no longer effective. Advertisers would not go to the expense of providing television commercials if they did not pay, that is, yield results in profits. But, evidently, researchers have found that people see enough, as the commercials go by at a fast pace, to identify the products being sold to the consumer. Seeing things, however briefly, is still a way the brain takes in information it might need to know. If it does not think it will need it, it will sift through the extraneous information, and you will dream about it, according to some researchers, at night when the brain is sweeping the landscape clean (The Diagram Group, 1982, pp. 208–209; Jensen, 1998, pp. 24–25).

"To see is to understand." We must definitely keep that in mind, and in our teaching plans, as we work with the youngsters of the present and the future.

If you do not consider yourself computer-savvy, but just a *user*, remember, "Where there's a will, there's a way," to quote my mother. Office stores sell plastic rulers and protractors or other templates that sport cut-outs of ovals, circles in various sizes, squares, triangles, and such: just what you need for quickly putting the parts of speech where you want them for classroom practice or old-time transparencies.

If you have computer programs like MacDraw, you can quickly learn to manipulate those shapes in various sizes and placements for culture boxes and event frames. I know it is a cliché, but "if I can do it, you can too." My sister lettered first-grade charts for our mother when she started teaching first grade. Find a student with artistic talent or neat lettering skills. And we all have students who seem to be born with computer skills. Use them. They'll love being needed.

So where do we go from here? Schooling is more than drilling basic concepts. What do you do with the information about maps, descriptions, writing paragraphs, grammar basics, and cultures once students know what they mean? That is the time when you will still find the teaching activities or strategies that work, the way teachers always used to find them: colleagues, teachers' professional journals, books, workshops, and conferences. Some ideas you will still create on your own. After all, who knows best what your students need?

One book with a telling title is *For the Learners' Sake: Brain-based Instruction for the 21st Century* (Stevens and Goldberg, 2001). The cover included the statements, "A Practical Guide to Transform Your Classroom and School; Discover the benefits of research on the brain and learning; Increase student achievement; Create flexible thinkers." Authors Judy Stevens and Dee Goldberg spend most of the book describing the brain, developing instruction compatible with the brain, student and teacher roles, and some mental models.

But for those teachers who want to share a bit of the brain's structure with their students, the authors include Nancy Marguiles' (*Mapping Inner Spaces*, 1991) way of using the hands to make fists representing the brain's hemispheres and lobes, and to locate the various processing areas, like the visual and audio centers and what they do. But they also get to chapters dealing with "Brain-Compatible Teaching Ideas" and "Strategies."

In chapter seven (p. 99), they remind their readers that ideas for the classroom ". . .must be used within a larger context of brain-compatible instructions . . . Your classroom must exhibit qualities present in a brain-compatible environment. These characteristics include real-life experiences, absence of threat, collaboration, positive emotional climate, and an understanding that each brain is unique. . . ." Later in chapter eight, they mention the familiar K-W-L, where students or whole classes list what they *know* about a topic, what they *want* to find out, and then what they actually *learned* (p. 109). That builds directly on the way the brain stores associated information. They recommend activities and projects, hands-on-learning, having an inquiry-based classroom, using graphic organizers and literature circles, small-groups and teams, and my personal favorite because it was a tenet of my career: integrating instruction.

I attended a panel discussion by four high school students at one of the Northern Virginia Council for Gifted and Talented Education conferences early in the 1980s. A girl on the panel impressed me when she said the thing she found most frustrating was when something in an art class prompted her to ask a question in her history class, and the teacher said, "Save that for next week. We'll hit that topic then."

Any book on brain research and any television documentary that includes testing situations will show video clips of researchers presenting various stimuli to the subjects, and the screen will show the sections—not a single location, but the sections of the brain that all respond at the same time. We will not get into the differences in reactions in males versus females here, but the idea that the brain activates various areas to respond to the same stimulus suggests that we are definitely using the whole brain when we think and learn. One idea will elicit an association or several associations and the connections will deepen thinking and learning. School subjects never remain in isolation.

Another influence for integrating curricula came from Dr. Joyce Van-Tassel-Baska, when she joined the faculty at William and Mary College in Williamsburg, Virginia. She held a conference on teaching gifted students that I attended. I know I cannot resurrect the date in my memory (1990?), but I have never forgotten that, in an address to the conferees, Dr. VanTassel-Baska mentioned that we should not overlook the arts in working with very able students. That holds for all students, really.

Taking a local field trip, "Cave-Man Day in the Park," recreating medieval society during a study of the Middle Ages, all provide social situations to strengthen learning at the same time that they are creating many associations between the curriculum topics. Correlating topics across subject areas requires careful timing and checking with colleagues; but imagine reading Greek and Roman mythology in language arts class during a social studies unit on those ancient cultures, while the science teacher is approaching astronomy through a bit of astrology— the zodiac signs of ancient Greeks—that relate to constellations and back to the myths. Math class might focus on Greek mathematicians.

Themes connect topics and subject areas and engage the whole brain in a way that reinforces the curricula content and allows students to find their own favorite interests as well. Keep your students relaxed and engaged, as they say, so that they learn more and like what they are doing. You will feel less of an automaton and enjoy your career, too. I hope my sharing of this brain-based approach to teaching will inspire and energize all the readers who have chosen to help children learn and prosper.

Winchester, Virginia
Fall 2006

Writing the last page of the first draft is the most enjoyable moment in writing. It's one of the most enjoyable moments in life, period.

—Nicholas Sparks, author (1965–)

NOTES

INTRODUCTION (NOTE I)

1. In the Introduction, I described Jane Healy's survey of cognitive scientists, neuroscientists, and psychologists, asking about the structural changes the brain might have undergone as the result of being bombarded by visual stimuli in the form of video games, videotapes, movies, and television for a quarter of a century. In the April 2007 issue of the University of Virginia's *Arts and Sciences Bulletin*, Associate Professor of Film Studies, Walter Korte, has an article on "Visual Thinking." He identifies the means by which we watch movies today, saying:

> "Students grow up in a world of multimedia images of which film is just one example. With the advent of digital technologies . . . We routinely watch films on numerous kinds of 'screens' in diverse formats, in varied venues and contexts . . . Given the universal availability of films, the smaller screens on which they are watched, and the stop-and-go control that the watcher exercises over them . . . A film has become less an experience than an object to be placed in a home-viewing apparatus or accessed on a computer and looked at in a casual, often piecemeal, manner . . . as we watch more movies on video screens and computers, our patterns of looking often decrease visibility."

Dr. Korte concluded with a quote from D. W. Griffith, uttered when the film director began his career in 1908: "The task I'm trying to achieve is above all to make you see."

Helping students to develop a visual concept model (a pattern) from several specific examples requires that they look closely and intently, finding details and analyzing them, and making comparisons. It involves direct, whole-class teaching, which means the instructor can be sure that student visibility is not decreased.

CHAPTER 3 (NOTE 2)

2. The late Kurt Vonnegut, in his last book, *A Man without a Country*, titled his third chapter, "Here's a lesson in creative writing" (pp. 24–37). While I am not in agreement with all he asserts, his two-axis visual for a story plan is so simple that it is simply ingenious. He instructs his readers to draw a vertical axis to the left of the paper and label it G at the top and I at the bottom. This represents a range of Good Fortune to Ill Fortune established at the start of the story. A horizontal axis begins midway on the fortune line and represents average stability. It is labeled B for "Beginning" and E for "Entropy," to quote Mr. Vonnegut. The plot line is drawn beginning at a relative point on the Good-to-Ill Fortune line and slips, slides, or plummets as low as the problems of the hero or heroine take it. As things improve, the line can rise suddenly, or in stair steps, or slope up and down like waves under a boat in a second grader's drawing. The chapter discusses variations of this story line from *Cinderella* to Shakespeare's *Hamlet*. Mr. Vonnegut suggests it is a way to plan one's creative writing effort, but he also proves it is helpful for analyzing literary forms.

CHAPTER 5 (NOTE 3)

3. Imagine my shock when, in trying to chase down the copyright holder for the poem about the parts of speech in chapter seven, I found a website for *Time* magazine articles that had one about a new grammar handbook (September 26, 1938). That delighted me; what shocked me

was a reference to: "Sentences have stop and go signals: a capital letter at the beginning is a green light; a dash, comma, semicolon or colon is a yellow light to make readers hesitate; a period, question mark or exclamation point is a red light." I thought I had that original idea. I guess instead of original, it was just logical, and I was not the first person to think of it.

CHAPTER 7 (NOTES 4–6)

4. Students who plan to take other languages in high school and college will need to understand the use of *persons* in the context of suffixes for the various foreign language grammars. Words add and change endings, suffixes, for differing reasons. Even in discussions of literature, we talk about stories and fiction books written *in the first person* or *in the third person*. You can make a personal decision to have students use their imaginations, or you can draw enough of a room on the chalkboard and add stick figures.

For those who choose the chalkboard drawing, just make a large rectangle to represent a classroom wall. Another tall and narrow rectangle can be the door. Do not forget a circle for the doorknob.

Tell the class to imagine they came to school a little early and went straight to the classroom, but found no one there, not even the teacher. Draw a stick figure. Say, "You are the first person in the classroom for a change; what might you say?" Hope that students will say something like, "Hey! I'm the first person here today!" Print that in a speech balloon.

Not far to the right of the first stick figure, draw a second one. Ask the class what they might say to the person who comes in next. You are looking for sentences that include the idea of being the first, but here is the second person. "I was first today, but I am surely glad to see you! It's weird to be in an empty classroom." You call the class's attention to the first person's calling him or herself *I*, and addressing the second person as *you*. Suggest that these two students were talking for a while and did not notice another student arrive and quietly start working at a desk— or if you do not want to take time to draw furniture, have them look out a window; you can draw a window quickly. Again, ask what the first two students would say about the third.

If the class comes up with something like, "What is he doing?" you are ready to chart the information. Make the familiar *Singular* and *Plural* columns side by side.

Write 1, 2, and 3 for first, second, and third persons, and fill in *I, you, he-she-or-it* on the left-, and *we, you, they* in the right-hand column.

For upper grades, ask students to "imagine arriving early at school and coming to your classroom to find no one there, not even the teacher." And proceed the same way without stopping to draw anything. At least the students are seeing images in their minds.

Just take time to define the three persons, and let students copy the drawing in their notebooks. The first person, referring to him or herself as *I*, is the speaker. The second person, the one spoken to, is addressed as *you*. And when people refer to persons outside their conversations, the people spoken about are the *third persons*. You can teasingly call that gossip.

There are choose-your-own-adventure books that upper-elementary and middle school students adore. They are written in the second person. They tell the reader, "You are standing at the door of the cottage. You hear the yelling inside. What do you do?" Then two options are given and page numbers where the reader can continue with the story following his or her choice for the plot-shift.

5. One of the two middle school librarians with whom I worked was a classics scholar who also taught Latin. When I began using the grammar symbols and sentence patterns, he employed them in his Latin course as well. He felt applying the same patterns in other classes created a consistency for students that supported further understanding.

The ideal situation is consistent use of the same patterns across subject areas, where possible and across grade levels. When the same patterns are introduced in early grades, they can be displayed in classrooms at higher grade levels and just need reviews or reminders, occasional references to the concepts. There was a term in the late twentieth century, *articulation*, which referred to teachers in the same subject area meeting across grade levels to make sure curriculum concepts were presented and developed as students moved through schools. Deciding on which concepts to teach when allows any unnoticed holes in the curriculum to be corrected.

Great Seneca Creek Elementary School, the first school awarded the Leadership in Energy and Environmental Design (LEED) certification in Maryland, received a gold rating by the U.S. Green Building Council for its environmentally friendly planning and construction (Edmundson, 2007). The newspaper article included a photo of a wall mural in a school stairwell: The Water Cycle. Now that is a real-life example of making concepts visible for all students.

6. Efforts were made to locate the copyright holder for *Around the Corner* through WorldCat, the Library of Congress, Johns Hopkins and Duke Universities, and the website www.kididdles.com. All were unsuccessful. Most used a Sergeant Major instead of a Yankee soldier, and had minor variations in melody line and lyrics. One version claimed the "Sergeant Major made love to me," which would certainly distract from the concept of prepositional phrases; and another involved high school teachers noting that students ran away from their questions, as found in *Gather 'Round: The Complete Community Song Book* by Walter Ehret, (1964, p. 37). The website indicated that author and composer were unknown. The community song book called it *traditional* and an *American Fun Song*.

A high school Advanced Placement English teacher told me that she always used the old Thanksgiving Holiday song, "Over the River and through the Woods." That solves everything, except that the song lacks the teasing element of: "Who do you think would marry you?" Take your pick.

REFERENCES

Abrahamson, E., and Freedman, D. H. (2006). *A Perfect Mess: The Hidden Benefits of Disorder.* New York: Little, Brown and Company.

Australian News and Information Bureau. (n.d.). *Your Colouring Book of Australian Birds and Animals.* Canberra, ACT: Paramac Printers.

Casagrande, June. (2006). *Grammar Snobs Are Great Big Meanies: Guide to Language for Fun and Spite.* New York: Penguin Group.

Diagram Group. (1982). *The Brain: A User's Manual.* New York: Berkley Books.

Edmundson, G. (2007). "At Great Seneca Creek, Being 'Green' Is Elementary," Outlook Section, *Washington Post*, May 13, p. B-8.

Ehret, W. (1964). *Gather 'Round: The Complete Community Song Book.* New York: Frank Music Corp, p. 37.

Ellsworth, P. C. and Sindt, V. G. (1994). "Helping 'Aha' to Happen: The Contributions of Irvine Sigel" *Educational Leadership* (February): pp. 40–41.

Florey, Kitty Burns (2006). *Sister Bernadette's Barking Dog: The Quirky History and Lost Art of Diagramming Sentences.* Hoboken, NJ: Melville House Publishing.

Fulton, J. L. (1986). *Developmental Teaching: Workbook 1.* Richmond, VA: Developmental Skills Institute.

Grun, B. (1978). *Timetables of History*, A Touchstone Book (Translated from German). New York: Simon and Schuster.

Healy, J. (1990). *Endangered Minds.* New York: Simon and Schuster.

———. (1987). *Your Child's Growing Brain.* New York: Doubleday.

Heyerly, D. (1996). *Visual Tools for Constructing Knowledge*. Alexandria, VA: Association for Supervision and Curriculum Development (ASCD).

Hunt, M. (1982). *The Universe Within: A New Science Explores the Human Mind*. New York: Simon and Schuster.

Jensen, E. (1998). *Teaching with the Brain in Mind*. Alexandria, VA.: ASCD.

Korte, W. (2007). "Visual Thinking." *Arts and Sciences Bulletin of University of Virginia*, 75 (April) p. 17.

Lemonick, Michael D. (2007). "The flavor of memories," *Time*, January 29.

Levine, E. (1998). *If You Lived with the Iroquois*. New York: Scholastic.

"Living Grammar" (1938). *Time*. September 26. Available at: www.time.com/time/magazine/article/0,9171,788821,00.html?iid=chix-sphere.

Lowery, L. (1998). "How new science curriculums reflect brain research: Advances in neuroscience contribute to the development of curriculums that build on the way the brain constructs knowledge." *Educational Leadership* (November) pp. 26–30.

Marceri, D. (2004). "Does bilingualism make you smarter?" *People's Weekly World*. January 8. www.pww.org/article/articleprint/4606/

Mulroy, D. (2003). *The War Against Grammar*. Portsmouth, NH: Boynton/Cook Publishers.

Norman, D. (1982). *Learning and Memory*. New York: Freeman and Co.

Slung, M. (1965). *The Absent-Minded Professor's Memory Book*. New York: Ballantine.

Sprenger, M. (1999). *Learning and Memory: The Brain in Action*. Alexandria, VA: ACDA.

Springer, S. P., and Deutsch, G. (1981). *Left Brain, Right Brain*. San Francisco: W. H. Freeman.

Stevens, J., and Goldberg, D. (2001). *For the Learners' Sake: Brain-Based Instruction for the 21st Century*. Tucson, AZ: Zephyr Press.

Vonnegut, K. (2007). *A Man without a Country*. D. Simon, ed. New York: Random House.

VosSavant, M. (2006). "Ask Marilyn." *Parade Magazine*, September 24, p. 26.

Thoreau, H. D. (1951). *Walden*. New York: Bramhall House.

Wallis, C. (2004). "What makes teens tick?" *Time*, March 10, pp. 57–65.

Warriner, J., Mersand, J., Townsend, H., and Griffith, F. (1973). *English Grammar and Composition: Fifth Course*. New York: Harcourt Brace Jovanovich.

Watson, W. and Nolte, J. M. (1955). *A Living Grammar*. St. Paul: Itasca Press, Webb Publishing.

ABOUT THE AUTHOR

Madlon T. Laster did her undergraduate work at Maryville College in Tennessee (1956). She taught in Wooster, Ohio, and at Community School in Tehran, Iran, before working on her Masters (1967) at George Peabody College for Teachers, now part of Vanderbilt University, in Nashville, Tennessee, while teaching in the Nashville-Davidson County School System. She and her husband lived in Beirut, Lebanon from 1967–1973, during which time she taught methods courses, a children's literature course, and supervised student teachers at Beirut College for Women, now Lebanese American University. She completed her forty-two-year teaching career in Winchester City Schools, Winchester, Virginia, in the city's middle school, and earned her Ph.D. from George Mason University (1996). Her certificate in cognitive instruction (1987) was earned through Radford University in Virginia.

Dr. Laster spent her career with the practical, or applied side, of instruction rather than publishing. She presented workshops in Zahle, Lebanon, and traveled with Dr. Julinda AbuNasr of the B.C.W. faculty to lead workshops on children's literature and libraries in Cairo, Egypt; Amman, Jordan; AbuDhabi, UAE; and Bahrain. Following the workshops in December 1985 and January 1986, Dr. AbuNasr and Dr. Laster collaborated on a book about establishing children's libraries, which was published in Arabic. She has also made presentations with colleagues at various conferences in Virginia, and faculty workshops in Bristol and Warrenton. This is her first book.

Dr. Laster may be reached at web site: Madlonlaster.com
Or through e-mail: mtlaster@mac.com